PRACTICAL ACCOUNTING FUNDAMENTALS™

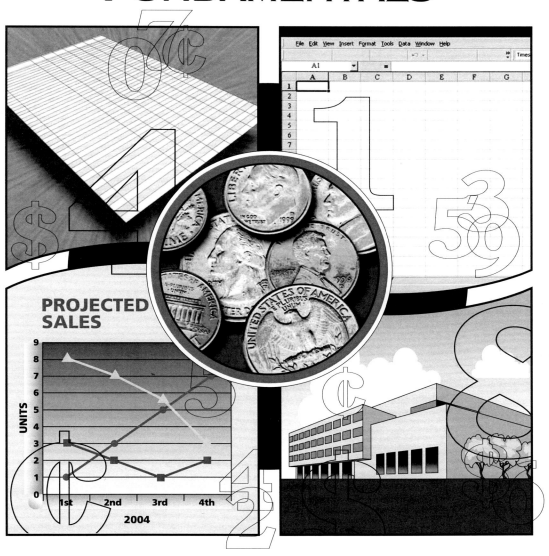

PROJECTED SALES

Melvin G. Peterman

INSIGHT™ TECHNICAL EDUCATION

WRITTEN BY LORI PETERMAN

First edition

ISBN 0-9722058-7-X

Edited by Mel Peterman
Designed by Mel Peterman
Cover & chapter title illustrations by Paul Bunch
Published by Melvin G. Peterman
www.insightteched.com
877-640-2256

Insight™, Insight™ Technical Education, insightteched.com™, insighttechnicaleducation.com™, sixbranches.com™, and Practical Accounting Fundamentals™ are trademarks of Melvin G. Peterman. All other trademarks belong to their respective owners.

Printed and assembled in the U.S.A.

It is the mark of an educated mind to be able to entertain a thought without accepting it.

~ Aristotle

Education is what survives when what has been learned has been forgotten.

~ B. F. Skinner

Contents

Forward

Practical Accounting Funamentals demonstrates our continued commitment to provide useful educational materials. These materials are for the person who wants to learn technical and professional subjects at home or on their own time. Practical Accounting Fundamentals can be used in helping to find a career path or in adding to life skills. It is our first book outside of the realm of technical art and drafting. We think that accounting and understanding business is critical in all career pursuits. Accounting is a topic that seems to be misunderstood and misrepresented on an on-going basis, yet business cannot exist without it. Practical Accounting Fundamentals takes the student step by step through the process of business accounting.

As with all of the products developed under the Insight Technical Education brand, Practical Accounting Fundamentals gets to the point fast to help you learn what you need in the minimum amount of time.

The author of Practical Accounting Fundamentals is Lori Peterman. Lori is my wife and our accountant, and she homeschools our four children. Lori has a BS in Accounting from Central Washington University and she has passed the CPA exam. Lori made a decisive career choice not to pursue the work that would have fulfilled the CPA requirements. Lori has worked for both large and small companies and has built several accounting systems from scratch for our own businesses over the years.

I think that you will appreciate the head-on approach that she takes in Practical Accounting Fundamentals. In our attempt to present this subject with clarity and brevity, there is no fluff in this book. Like all of our materials, this is not the end of your studies should you decide to follow accounting as a career path. Practical Accounting Fundamentals is meant to give you some tools, to open your eyes to the world of business, and to allow you to get your feet wet. When you have completed this book, you will have a greater understanding of accounting, bookkeeping, and business information. You will also know the basics of setting up an accounting system from the beginning. The learning you do here will last a lifetime.

Relax, learn, and enjoy.

Melvin G. Peterman
Editor and Publisher
Insight Technical Education

Introduction

$\div X \, {}^x_\div \!{}^+_\div \, {}^-_\div X \!{}^-_- \!{}^+_\div \, {}^-_\div \!{}^+_\div \, X \, {}^-_\div \!{}^+_\div \, {}^\div_X$

P ractical Accounting Funamentals has been clearly written to help clarify what accounting really is and why it is so important. This book brings accounting principles down to earth so that it is understandable and goes directly to the point. All information is relevant and is a building block for what follows. Accounting is a fundamental tool of business, whether you want to start a micro business or you would like to work in a Fortune 100 company.

Practical Accounting Fundamentals is written as a self-teaching, self-paced, step-by-step instruction guide. Each chapter has a fundamental lesson that is clearly written out and includes both demonstrated examples and practice problems to ensure understanding. At the completion of the book, you will have a clear understanding of what accounting is and what accounting is not. You may decide to follow accounting as a career path or it may be a subject that will be used to benefit you in life and to deepen your understanding of business.

You will begin with an overview of several different types of financial statements. This will familiarize you with how to gather the information and the format that it needs to be presented in. After starting with simple financial statements, you will end up creating a complete set of books.

Accounting is rarely done by hand with paper and pencil anymore. Instead, it is done using accounting software on the computer, which can range from simple spreadsheets to programs such as QuickBooks® or Peachtree® to complex custom software.

What you need:
• 4-column ledger paper (ignore columns when you don't need them all)
• 10-key printing calculator (this is a basic piece of office equipment and can be easily learned on your own with some practice; knowing how to run a 10-key by touch is as important as knowing how to type by touch)
• If you prefer, you may use a computer and a spreadsheet program like Lotus®1-2-3® or Microsoft®Excel. There are also free/cheap spreadsheet programs available on the Internet.

Additional instructions – Do the problems for each chapter as many times as necessary to feel comfortable with your mastery of the information.

Where is there dignity unless there is honesty?
~ Cicero

What is Accounting?

Accounting and bookkeeping are part of the accounting information system. This information system is used to provide financial data to those who need to make decisions about a company. All individuals and companies use accounting and/or bookkeeping for record keeping, financial decisions, taxes, etc. The bookkeeper records the data describing the financial activities of the company in journals and ledgers. The bookkeeper also reconciles and maintains these records. This information can then be put into a report form, which varies depending on the decision-maker's needs. The most common of these reports are the financial statements such as the balance sheet and the income statement. The financial statements are intended primarily for external users, such as investors and government agencies. Internal users, primarily management, use these reports in addition to classified reports that may contain information not intended for use outside the business. In addition to the production of financial statements, the accountant analyzes and interprets the financial data and accounts of the company for management as well as making sure that the accounting for the transactions and the resulting reports follow GAAP. In a small business, often there is only one person who is both bookkeeper and accountant.

Generally accepted accounting principles (GAAP) are the principles on which the procedures utilized in accounting are based. These principles have evolved over time because they are generally accepted by the accounting profession as proper at the present time. Changes occur due to the changing business and technological environment and from trying to determine what is the best way to accurately report on the financial activities of business.

GAAP are not conveniently all written down in one place. However, there are some books that attempt to give reference to GAAP in one place, such as <u>Wiley GAAP 2003: Interpretations and Applications of GAAP 2003</u> and <u>Miller GAAP Guide 2003</u>. Primarily GAAP are a collection of statements, interpretations, guides, etc., put out by several groups. These groups include the following:

> The Financial Accounting Standards Board (FASB) issues pronouncements. It, along with its predecessors, the Accounting Principles Board and the Committee on Accounting Procedure, has probably provided the most GAAP and is the primary source of GAAP.

> The American Institute of Certified Public Accountants (AICPA) is the national professional organization for certified public accountants. They issue Interpretations, Audit Guides, Accounting Guides, and Statements of Position.

> The Securities and Exchange Commission (SEC) regulations also influence GAAP since publicly traded corporations must follow them when filing financial reports with the SEC.

> The Internal Revenue Service (IRS) regulations affect GAAP when accounting methods that are required for reporting to the IRS are also used in financial accounting.

Much of GAAP is learned as accounting is learned. Rather than studying GAAP by itself, the principles are applied to each subject as it is learned. For example, which financial statements to prepare and how they are prepared are part of GAAP. For more complex issues, the above sources (and others) are consulted.

Knowledge of technology is also important to accountants and bookkeepers. In addition to being familiar with accounting software, you must be aware of other uses of technology. Spreadsheets are used for tracking and reporting on some items, word processing programs are needed for creating reports and other communications, email and time tracking software are used to keep you informed and organized, databases are used to track information and create reports, and the list goes on. We have entered the technology age where there is always something new to learn and utilize. Regardless of what direction your life is headed in, being familiar with the technology available is valuable.

Questions:

1. What is the accounting information system?

2. What is accounting?

3. How is accounting used?

1. accounting + book keeping, the system is used to keep track of buying, spending and money made. the accounting info system is used to keep records

2. remembering, recording, and reporting money spent and earned

3. accounting can be used to back-up/support taxes,

2

Whenever you are asked if you can do a job, tell 'em, "Certainly, I can!" Then get busy and find out how to do it.
~ Theodore Roosevelt

The Balance Sheet

In this chapter, and the next three, there will be an example of a financial statement along with some explanation and definitions to get you started. We will assume that the companies we will be talking about are corporations. In Chapter 20, we will discuss the various forms of business that are commonly found and the differences in accounting for them. We will use the ABC Supply Company's financial statements for the year 2002 for these four chapters.

Here is an example of a balance sheet. The current assets are totaled and then added to the total of the long-term assets to give us total assets. Likewise, the current liabilities are totaled and added to the total of the stockholders' equity to give us total equities. Total equities and total assets must be equal.

ABC Supply Company
Balance Sheet
December 31, 2002

Assets			Equities		
Current assets:			Current liabilities:		
Cash	$13,000		Accounts payable	$15,500	
Accounts receivable	9,500		Salaries payable	3,000	$18,500
Inventory	10,000	$32,500			
			Stockholders' equity:		
Long-term investment:			Capital stock, 2700 shares		
Investment in land		15,000	issued & outstanding	$27,000	
		$47,500	Retained earnings	2,000	29,000
					$47,500

It is customary to put a dollar sign beside the first amount in each column and beside an amount appearing below an underline. It is also customary to list detail figures in a column with the total to the right of the last item. Final totals are double underlined.

The balance sheet shows a picture of the business at a particular moment in time. It tells you what the assets of the business are, its liabilities, and the owners' (stockholders') equity. The balance sheet is always "in balance", i.e., the assets always equal the equities.

Assets

Let's discuss the elements of the balance sheet. Assets are future economic benefits that the business owns the rights to. Assets are considered to provide future economic benefits for a number of reasons, which include the following:

1. The asset may have purchasing power. Cash is an example; other assets may be acquired with it.
2. The asset is a claim for money. Accounts receivable is an example.
3. The asset can be sold in order to gain cash. Merchandise inventory is an example.
4. The asset offers potential services. Buildings, land, machinery, and equipment are examples.

The primary asset categories are:
Current assets
Long-term investments
Property, plant, and equipment
Intangible assets
Other assets

Current assets are those assets which can be used in the short term. This includes cash, temporary investments, accounts and notes receivable, inventory, supplies, and prepayments that will be used or will expire within a normal operating cycle. The operating cycle is the flow of cash to inventory, to receivables, and back to cash. The time this takes varies from industry to industry. As a general rule, short term equals one year or less.

Long-term investments are any investments that can't be considered short-term, i.e., held for over one year. These would include land held for resale and investment in the stock of other companies.

Property, plant, and equipment includes land, buildings, equipment, etc., used in the operations of the business and not intended to be sold. Some examples are: parking lots, office equipment, furniture, machinery, and delivery equipment.

Intangible assets are noncurrent assets that do not have physical substance. Examples of these are patents, copyrights, franchises, and goodwill. Goodwill is the value placed on a company for its ability to produce more income than its competitors. This is due to many factors which can include locations, quality of employees, or reputation.

Other assets are any assets that do not fit into any other classification. An example of this is land being held for a future building site.

Equities

Liabilities, on the other hand, are economic obligations of the business. These arise from various activities of the business, such as purchasing inventory on credit.

The primary equity categories are:
Liabilities:
    Current liabilities
    Long-term liabilities
Stockholders' equity (also called owners' equity)

Current liabilities are debts or obligations that are expected to be paid in the current operating cycle or one year. Some examples include: accounts payable, short-term notes payable, and taxes payable. The excess of current assets over current liabilities is referred to as working capital. The ratio of current assets to current liabilities is the current ratio. These figures reflect the ability of the company to meet its short-term obligations since the current assets are used to pay the current liabilities.

Long-term liabilities are liabilities not classified as short-term. These include bonds issued and mortgages.

Stockholders' equity is defined by the source of the equity. Capital stock is the investment by stockholders. Retained earnings are the earnings of the company. The excess of the assets over the liabilities is the owners' equity. Using the balance sheet on the previous page:

Assets	$47,500
Liabilities	-18,500
Owners' equity	$29,000

ABC Supply Company in the above example has a strong financial position. Its current assets are greater than its current liabilities. The cash balance seems reasonable compared to the other current assets and current liabilities. The long-term investment can be turned into cash if circumstances require it. Lastly, the company has no long-term debt.

Questions:

1. What is a balance sheet?
   a record for co's assets, liabilities and owners equity

✗ 2. What are assets?
   Something a business owns - cash, inventory, supplies, equipment

✗ 3. What are liabilities?
   Something a business owes - paying employees, supplies unpayed for

✗ 4. What is owners' equity?
   owners equity is your right to your assets - liabilities

Problems:

A. Fill in the missing numbers (the information for Why Knot Corporation is going to be used for this problem and problem A in the next three chapters):

Why Knot Corporation
Balance Sheet
December 31, 2002

Assets
Current assets:

Cash	$10,000	
Accounts receivable	11,500	
Inventory	8,000	$A *29500*

Long-term assets:

Land	$6,000	
Building	B *13500*	19,500
		$ C *49000*

Equities
Current liabilities:

Accounts payable	$13,500	
Salaries payable	D *3000*	
Taxes payable	3,500	$20,000

Stockholders' equity:

Capital stock	$18,000	
Retained earnings	E *11000*	29,000
		$49,000

[Handwritten column, labeled "ac pay."]
9800
6076
375
7663
6076
5335
8330

2500 - Sal. pay
0 - taxes

95000

B. Given the following information, create a balance sheet for 2001 (make up your own company name).

95000 Cash - $36,000   *28500* Accounts payable - $21,000
       Accounts receivable - $27,000   Salaries payable - $7,500
       Inventory - $32,000   *192500* Capital stock - $150,000
126000 Land - $54,000   Retained earnings - $42,500
       Building - $72,000

clutch eggs
balance sheet
December 31 2001

Assets
Current assets
cash $36000
account receivable 27000
inventory   32000   *$95000*

long-term assets
land $54000
building   72000   *$126000*
                          $221,000

Equities
Current liabilities
accounts payable $21000
salaries payable   7500 $28500
Taxes payable

Stockholders equity
capital stock $150000
retained earnings 42500 $192500
                            $192500
                            $221000

Our character is what we do when we think no one is looking.
~ H. Jackson Brown, Jr.

The Income Statement

All businesses want to produce net income (sometimes referred to as earnings or profit) from their business activities. This information is shown on the income statement. Net income is the excess of revenues (assets coming in) over expenses (cost of goods or services used in order to generate income – assets going out). An excess of expenses over revenues results in a net loss. Revenues and expenses will be discussed further in chapter 10.

Below is an example of an income statement. We start with sales and then subtract the total of all expenses to determine net income (or loss).

ABC Supply Company
Income Statement
For the Year Ended December 31, 2002

Revenue:		
Sales of merchandise		$83,000
Deduct expenses:		
Cost of goods sold	$51,000	
Salaries expense	17,500	
Rent expense	6,000	
Other expense	4,000	78,500
Net income		$4,500
Earnings per share ($4,500 ÷ 2,700 shares issued)		$1.67

Some of the common uses of the income statement include:

1. Included in report to stockholders to be used in determining the financial position of the company.
2. Submitted to a financial institution in support of a request for a loan.
3. Used by investors to determine whether to buy or sell shares of stock.
4. Used by management in decision-making in a wide variety of areas, such as detecting trends, determining whether to expand production, change advertising, add a new product, etc.

For any of the above uses, the balance sheet is also examined. The balance sheet and income statement are supplemental to each other.

Exercises - 3

Questions:

1. What is an income statement?

   a statement that shows a companies income and expenses

2. What is net income?

   the money a company has left after taxes, paying employee, and cost of goods

3. What are revenues?

   cash coming in

4. What are expenses?

   money spent on something - assets going out

Problems:

A. Fill in the missing numbers:

Why Knot Corporation
Income Statement
For the Year Ended December 31, 2002

sub total - single line
grand total - double line

Revenue:		
Sales		$132,000
Deduct expenses:		
Cost of goods sold	$76,000	
Salaries expense	A - *30,600*	
Rent expense	9,000	
Miscellaneous expense	7,500	122,500
Net income		$ B - *9500*
Earnings per share (1000 shares issued)		$ C - *9.50*

B. Given the following information, create an income statement for 2008 (make up your own company name).

Sales - $293,000
Cost of goods sold - $175,000
Salaries expense - $59,000
Rent expense - $12,000
Other expense - $10,500
1500 shares were issued

Action springs not from thought, but from a readiness for responsibility.
~ Dietrich Bonhoeffer

Statement of Retained Earnings

Retained earnings are part of the stockholders' equity, reflecting the profitable operations of the business. Retained earnings equals the accumulation of net income minus any net losses and paid dividends to date. In the example below, the company began operating in 2002, which is why the beginning retained earnings are $0. In all future years, the retained earnings at the end of the year become the beginning retained earnings of the next year. Starting with retained earnings as of January 1, we add net income for the year (or subtract a net loss). From that total, we subtract dividends to determine retained earnings as of December 31.

ABC Supply Company
Statement of Retained Earnings
For the Year Ended December 31, 2002

Retained earnings, January 1, 2002	$0
Net income for 2002	4,500
Total	$4,500
Deduct dividends	2,500
Retained earnings, December 31, 2002	$2,000

The retained earnings statement shows the changes that have taken place in retained earnings during the time period covered. One of the changes is the payment of dividends. Dividends are a payment (usually in cash) to stockholders as a result of profitable operations. Dividends are not an expense since they are not paid in order to generate revenue.

The retained earnings statement is generally included in the set of financial statements, but it is optional. Sometimes the statement is even combined with the income statement to produce a statement of income and retained earnings. This, however, is usually only seen in very large corporations.

Notice that the net income shown on the statement of retained earnings is the same as that on the income statement in the previous chapter. Also, the year-end retained earnings on this statement match the retained earnings shown on the example of a balance sheet in Chapter 2.

Exercises - 4

Questions:

1. What is a statement of retained earnings?

it shows the changes that have taken place in retained earnings during the time period covered

2. What are retained earnings?

Part of the stockholders equity. reflecting the profitable operations of the business

3. What are dividends?

are usually cash payments to stockholders as a result of profitable operations - they arnt expenses bc they arnt paid in order to generate revenue

Problems:

A. Fill in the missing numbers:

Why Knot Corporation
Statement of Retained Earnings
For the Year Ended December 31, 2002

Retained earnings, January 1, 2002	$ **A** - *3000*
Net income for 2002	9,500
Total	$12,500
Deduct dividends	1,500
Retained earnings, December 31, 2002	$ **B** - *14000*

B. Given the following information, create a statement of retained earnings for 2005 (make up your own company name).

Retained earnings on December 31, 2004 - $40,000
Net income for 2005 - $36,000
Dividends paid - $3,000

There is no failure except in no longer trying.
~ Elbert Hubbard

Statement of Cash Flow

The statement of cash flow is a report of financial management. It gives information on the investing and financing activities of the business for a period of time. In other words, on the use of the cash. This statement is not prepared from the cash account. It is prepared by analyzing the changes in assets and equities during the current period (the difference between the balance at the beginning of the year and the balance at the end of the year), since cash is affected at some point in time when assets and equities are increased and decreased. The cash provided from operations is the cash available to management for business operations and distribution (e.g., dividends). It is the excess of cash generated by revenue over cash used for expenses. To net income, we add and subtract the increases and decreases in the asset and equity accounts, since they also reflect the use of cash. Any depreciation or amortization would also be added in this section (these will be discussed in a future chapter). Increases in asset accounts are deducted from net income and decreases are added. Conversely, increases in equity accounts are added and decreases are subtracted. Think about it this way. When non-cash asset accounts (such as inventory) are increased, usually cash has been (or will be) decreased. Therefore, less cash is available. When liabilities are increased, cash has usually been retained (or even increased). Cash provided from other sources includes all other transactions that would increase cash, such as issuing stock or selling non-inventory assets. The cash applied includes uses of cash that don't apply directly to the normal operation of the business, such as purchasing land or other assets and payment of dividends. This statement also would include non-cash activity such as acquiring land by issuing long-term notes payable.

[handwritten: or liability]

Following is an example of a statement of cash flow. The adjustments due to operating activities are totaled and then added to (or subtracted from) net income. Any other cash provided from operations is then added. Next, we total the cash applied and subtract it from the total financial resources provided. This gives us the increase (or decrease, if negative) in cash for the period. The summary then takes the increase (or decrease) in cash and adds the cash balance from the beginning of the period to get the cash balance at the end of the period. (Note: parentheses around a number indicate that it is negative, or being subtracted.)

ABC Supply Company
Statement of Cash Flow
For the Year Ended December 31, 2002

Sources of financial resources:			
Cash provided from operations:			
Net income		$4,500	
Adjustments to reconcile net income to net cash provided by operating activities:			
Increase in Accounts receivable	$(9,500)		
Increase in Inventory	(10,000)		
Increase in Accounts payable	15,500		
Increase in Salaries payable	3,000	(1,000)	
Cash provided from operations for period		$3,500	
Cash provided from other sources:			
Issuance of capital stock *-t(2n I*		27,000	
Total financial resources provided for period			$30,500
Uses of financial resources:			
Cash applied:			
Purchase of land *-t(2n5 II*		$15,000	
Dividends paid *- 13*		2,500	
Total financial resources used for period			17,500
Increase in cash for period			$13,000
Summary:			
Increase in cash for period			$13,000
Cash balance at beginning of period			0
Cash balance at end of period			$13,000

[handwritten: - check figure]

Exercises – 5

Questions:

1. What is a statement of cash flow?
a report of financial management that gives info on investing and the financing activities of a business over a period of time.

2. What is cash provided from operations?
the section of a co's cash flow statement that represents the amount of $ a co consumes.

Problems:

A. Fill in the blanks:

Why Knot Corporation
Statement of Cash Flow
For the Year Ended December 31, 2002

Sources of financial resources:

Cash provided from operations: *– cash available to management.*

Net income		$9,500
Adjustments to reconcile net income to net cash provided by operating activities:		
Increase in Account receivable	$(1,700)	
Increase in Inventory	**A** *–(1500)*	
Increase in Accounts payable	2,500	
Increase in Salaries payable	500	
Decrease in Tax payable	(500)	**B** *–(700)*
Cash provided from operations for period		$8,800
Cash provided from other sources:		
Issuance of capital stock		3,000
Total financial resources provided for period		$ **C** *– 11,800*

Uses of financial resources:

Cash applied:		
Building	$ **D** *– 13,500*	
Dividends paid	1,500	
Total financial resources used for period		15,000
Increase (Decrease) in cash for period		$ **E** *– (3,200)*

Summary:

Increase (Decrease) in cash for period	$ **E** *–(3,200)*
Cash balance at beginning of period	**F** *– 13,200*
Cash balance at end of period	$10,000

B. Given the following information, create a statement of cash flow (make up your own company name).

Net income - $17,800
Increase in Accounts receivable - $13,500
Increase in Inventory - $8,000
Increase in Accounts payable - $17,000
Increase in Salaries payable - $3,000
Purchased van - $8,000
Paid dividends - $2,000
Cash balance at beginning of period - $18,000
Cash balance at end of period - $24,300

COGS – cost of goods sold
P&L – profit and loss

It is good to have an end to journey toward,
but it is the journey that matters in the end.
~ Ursula K. LeGuin

Transactions

Accounting is an economic information system. This system takes the economic data of a business and changes it into economic information. This transformation is called the accounting process. There are three steps in this process: 1) recording economic data as transactions, 2) classifying and summarizing this data at the end of a period of time, and 3) reporting and interpreting the information in the form of financial statements.

Transactions are economic events that change the assets or equities, or both, of the company. Transactions can be external or internal. External transactions are those which involve an exchange of assets or equities with entities outside the company. These include sale of shares of stock, sale of merchandise, purchase of inventory, and purchase of equipment. Internal transactions happen within the company. Some examples are expensing a long-term asset (depreciating or decreasing its value over time) and the expiration of a prepaid item (such as advertising or insurance).

The basic accounting equation can be stated as follows:

Assets = Equities

This can be expanded to show the components of equities:

Assets = Liabilities + Owner's equity
Assets = Liabilities + Capital stock + Retained earnings

Transactions affect the accounting equation because they reflect increases and decreases in assets and equities. Each transaction has a dual effect; it affects at least two items (it has two sides or parts), which maintains the equality between assets and equities. For example, if a company issues stock for $6,000, equities (stock) are increased and assets (cash) are increased by $6,000. This keeps the equation in balance. Similarly, if a company purchases equipment for $4,000 in cash, assets are increased (equipment) and decreased (cash) by $4,000. Transactions are therefore analyzed in terms of the accounting equation.

On the following page are some examples of transactions and the effect they have on the accounting equation.

2002 Transactions

		Assets	=	Equities

Transaction		Assets	Equities
1. Issued capital stock for cash, $27,000. - The company acquired $27,000 cash, an asset, and issued capital stock, $27,000 of stockholders equity.	Before Change After	$0- + 27,000 $27,000	$0- + 27,000 $27,000
2. Purchased land as a long-term investment for $15,000 cash. - The asset, land, was increased $15,000 but it was offset by a decrease in cash.	Before Change After	$27,000 + 15,000 -15,000 $27,000	$27,000 $27,000
3. Purchased merchandise on account for $61,000. - An asset, merchandise inventory, was created in the amount of $61,000 and accounts payable, a liability, was also created for the same amount.	Before Change After	$27,000 + 61,000 $88,000	$27,000 + 61,000 $88,000
4a. Merchandise was sold on credit for $83,000. - An asset, accounts receivable, was created and the sales revenue of $83,000 increased retained earnings.	Before Change After	$88,000 + 83,000 $171,000	$88,000 + 83,000 $171,000
4b. The merchandise sold and delivered to customers cost the company $51,000. - The asset, merchandise inventory, was decreased by $51,000 and retained earnings were decreased by the cost of goods sold.	Before Change After	$171,000 - 51,000 $120,000	$171,000 - 51,000 $120,000
5. $73,500 of the amount receivable from customers was received. - The asset, cash, was increased by $73,500 and the asset, accounts receivable, was decreased.	Before Change After	$120,000 + 73,500 - 73,500 $120,000	$120,000 $120,000
6. Paid $45,500 on amount owed for inventory. - The asset, cash, decreased and the liability, accounts payable, decreased $45,500.	Before Change After	$120,000 - 45,500 $74,500	$120,000 - 45,500 $74,500
7. Paid rent of $6,000. - The asset, cash, decreased by $6,000 and retained earnings was decreased by the rent expense of $6,000.	Before Change After	$74,500 - 6,000 $68,500	$74,500 - 6,000 $68,500
8. Paid miscellaneous expenses of $4,000. - Cash decreased $4,000 and expenses decreased retained earnings.	Before Change After	$68,500 - 4,000 $64,500	$68,500 - 4,000 $64,500
9a. Salaries of $14,500 were paid. - Cash and retained earnings decreased by $14,500.	Before Change After	$64,500 - 14,500 $50,000	$64,500 - 14,500 $50,000
9b. The salaries for December of $3,000 won't be paid until January. - A liability, salaries payable, increased by $3,000 and retained earnings decreased.	Before Change After	$50,000 $50,000	$50,000 + 3,000 - 3,000 $50,000
10. Paid dividends of $2,500. - Decreased cash and retained earnings by $2,500.	Before Change After	$50,000 - 2,500 $47,500	$50,000 - 2,500 $47,500

The above transactions can be summarized in a transaction worksheet. This is nothing more than an expansion of the basic accounting equation, Assets = Equities. See the next page for the transaction worksheet for these transactions.

ABC Supply Company
Transaction Worksheet
Year 2002

| | Assets | | | | = | Equities | | | Retained Earnings | | |
Explanation	Cash	+ Accounts Receivable	+ Merchandise Inventory	+ Land	=	Accounts Payable	+ Salaries Payable	+ Capital Stock	+ Revenues	- Expenses	= Balance
Beginning balances	0	0	0	0		0	0	0			0
1. Issued capital stock for cash	27,000							27,000			
2. Purchased land for cash	(15,000)			15,000							
3. Purchased merchandise on account (credit)			61,000			61,000					
4a. Sales on account		83,000							83,000		
4b. Cost of goods sold			(51,000)							(51,000)	
5. Cash receipts from customers	73,500	(73,500)									
6. Cash payment on account	(45,500)					(45,500)					
7. Paid rent	(6,000)									(6,000)	
8. Paid miscellaneous expenses	(4,000)									(4,000)	
9a. Salaries paid	(14,500)									(14,500)	
9b. Unpaid salaries owed							3,000			(3,000)	
10. Paid dividends	(2,500)										(2,500)
Ending balances	13,000	9,500	10,000	15,000	=	15,500	3,000	27,000			2,000
			47,500		=			47,500			

Exercises ~ 6

Questions:

1. What are transactions?
economic events that change the assets and/or equities of a co

2. What is the basic accounting equation?
assets = equities

Problems:

A. The results of the 2006 transactions of Dewy Ornott, Inc. are listed below.
Assume all beginning balances are zero. Produce a transaction worksheet. This can be done on ledger paper or in a spreadsheet.

1. The company was organized and capital stock was issued for $100,000.
2. Purchased merchandise on account for $120,000.
3a. Made cash sales of $97,000.
3b. Cost of goods sold was $60,000.
4. Paid advertising expenses of $2,000.
5. Paid rent for the year $12,000.
6a. Sales on account were $80,000.
6b. Cost of goods sold was $48,000.
7. Cash payments for salaries were $43,000.
8. Made payment on account of $100,000.
9. Received $75,000 from customers.
10. Owed salaries at year-end of $6,000.
11. Cash dividends of $4,000 were paid.

B. The results of the 2001 transactions of Smiling Onion Company are listed below. Assume all beginning balances are zero.
   1. Produce a transaction worksheet.
   2. Produce the 2001 balance sheet, statement of retained earnings, income statement, and statement of cash flow.

1. The company was organized and capital stock was issued for cash of $90,000.
2. Purchased merchandise for cash of $8,000.
3a. Made cash sales of $14,000.
3b. The cost of goods sold for cash was $5,500.
4. Purchased merchandise on account for $80,000.
5. Paid advertising expenses of $1,500.
6a. Sales of merchandise on account were $110,000.
6b. The cost of goods sold on account was $60,000.
7. Paid rent for the year of $7,500.
8. Cash payments for salaries were $16,000.
9. Received cash from customers in the amount of $80,000.
10. Made a cash payment for merchandise purchased on account of $40,000.
11. Land was acquired for a long-term investment for $20,000 cash.
12. At year end, the company owed $5,000 for unpaid salaries.
13. Paid cash dividends of $2,500.

Practical Accounting Fundamentals

7

Motivation is what gets you started. Habit is what keeps you going.
~ Unknown

Journal Entries & Accounts

The recording of economic data (transactions) as taught in the previous chapter can be accomplished in several ways. You can use ledger paper and pencil, spreadsheets (such as Excel or Lotus 1-2-3), or various types of accounting software (such as Quickbooks or Peachtree). It is important to understand the process involved in recording this information by hand so that if you do use a computer program, you know what is happening to the data you enter and whether the financial statements produced are reasonable or not.

Accounts

The transaction worksheet, while clearly showing the effect of each transaction, can quickly become cumbersome. In order to keep it manageable, a record is maintained for each asset and equity on the balance sheet. This record is called an account. The record for each account is kept in a ledger. Traditionally, each account record was kept on a piece of paper, called ledger paper, that was kept in a book, called the ledger. We still refer to the collection of the account records as a ledger, whether it's on paper or in a computer program. In the ledger, the account records are kept in financial statement order (assets, liabilities, stockholders' equity, revenues, and expenses). Before a transaction is recorded in each account in the ledger, a journal entry is made. The journal is a "book" that contains the record of each transaction of the company in chronological order. It is the first place this information is recorded. It lists the date, the accounts affected by the transaction, and the amounts. The entry for a particular transaction is called a journal entry.

In order to record a journal entry, you must know whether an account will be debited or credited. Debits and credits, as used in accounting, are different than you are probably used to thinking of them. Most people think of credits as a good thing, like an increase in their bank account. Likewise, debits are commonly thought of as a negative. Don't let this confuse you, because in accounting, increases in assets and decreases in equities are recorded as debits. These are recorded on the left side of the account, the "debit side." Decreases in assets and increases in equities are referred to as credits. These are recorded on the right side of the account, the "credit side." The difference between the total debits and the total credits recorded in an account is referred to as the account balance. If the debits are greater than the credits, the account is said to have a debit balance. Conversely, if the credits are greater than the debits, the account is said to have a credit balance. Asset accounts typically have debit balances and equity accounts usually have credit balances. This ties in with the form of the balance sheet showing the assets on the left and the equities on the right.

An example of the layout of a traditional account form follows:

Sheet No.				Account Title			Account No.	
Date	Explanation	Ref.	Amount	Date	Explanation	Ref.	Amount

The left side is used for debit entries and the right for credit. To simplify the illustration, the account form is often shown as follows:

Debit	Credit

This is referred to as a T-account because that is what it looks like.

The increase and decrease to accounts can be demonstrated with the T-account as follows.

Asset accounts (debit balance)

Debit (Dr.)		Credit (Cr.)
Balance	$xxx	Decrease
Increase		

Example of cash account activity:
        Beginning balance, $800
        Cash receipt, $450
        Cash disbursement, $300

Cash		
Balance	800	300 *dispursement*
recipts 450		

Equity accounts (credit balance)

Dr.	Cr.	
Decrease	Balance	$xxx
	Increase	

Example of accounts payable account activity:
        Beginning balance, $500
        Purchased merchandise on account, $350
        Payment to reduce accounts payable, $400

Accounts Payable		
payment 400	Balance	500
		350 *purchased*

To connect this back to the accounting equation, we see this:

Assets		=	Equities	
Debits	Credits	Debits		Credits
(increase)	(decrease)	(decrease)		(increase)

As discussed previously, the revenues and expenses of the company affect retained earnings. Revenues increase retained earnings and expenses decrease them. We could record these directly in the retained earning account but that would make it more difficult to put the information together for the income statement. Therefore, we have an account for each type of expense and each type of revenue. In order to remember which are debits and which are credits, think of revenues and expense as being branches of retained earnings. Since increases in retained earnings are recorded as credits, revenues are also recorded as credits. In the same way, since decreases in retained earnings are recorded as debits, expenses are also recorded as debits.

Retained Earnings	
Expenses decrease retained earnings and are a debit	Revenues increase retained earnings and are a credit
↓	↓

Expense Account		Revenue Account	
Expense is			Revenue is a
a debit			credit

Similar to expenses, dividends also decrease retained earnings. They are therefore recorded as debits in the dividend account. This account is also a subdivision of retained earnings.

This debit-credit plan results in the following normal account balances:

Debit Balance Accounts	Credit Balance Accounts
Assets	Liabilities
Expenses	Capital stock
Dividends	Retained earnings
	Revenues

The increases and decreases as shown through the accounting equation are as follows:

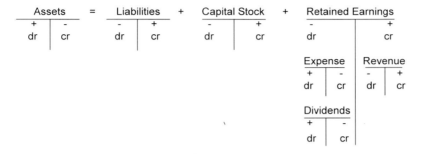

As discussed in Chapter 6, each transaction has a dual economic affect; it affects at least two items. Under the debit-credit plan, every transaction affects at least two accounts and total debits equal total credits for that transaction. Since the debits are equal to the credits in each transaction, the total of all debit entries are equal to the total of all credit entries. This system of debits and credits being equal is called double-entry accounting.

Journal Entries

The process of journalizing is the recording of each transaction in the journal. Following is the journal for ABC Supply Company for the year 2002. These transactions are taken from the examples used in the previous chapters, with dates arbitrarily assigned in order to show how the date is recorded. The debit amounts are always listed first, then the credit amounts. On the next line is an explanation of the transaction.

2002			debit	credit
Jan	2	Cash	27,000	
		Capital Stock		27,000
		Issued capital stock for cash		
	5	Land	15,000	
		Cash		15,000
		Purchased land for cash		
	10	Merchandise inventory	61,000	
		Accounts payable		61,000
		Purchased inventory on account		
Feb	4	Accounts receivable	83,000	
		Revenue		83,000
		Sales on account		
	4	Cost of goods sold	51,000	
		Merchandise inventory		51,000
		Cost of goods sold		
Mar	1	Cash	73,500	
		Accounts receivable		73,500
		Cash receipts from customers		
	15	Accounts payable	45,500	
		Cash		45,500
		Payment on account		
May	15	Rent expense	6,000	
		Cash		6,000
		Paid rent		
Oct	20	Miscellaneous expense	6,500	
		Cash		6,500
		Paid miscellaneous expenses		
Dec	1	Salaries expense	14,500	
		Cash		14,500
		Paid salaries		
	31	Salaries expense	3,000	
		Salaries payable		3,000
		Unpaid salaries owed		
	31	Dividends	2,500	
		Cash		2,500
		Paid dividends		

Sometimes transactions involve more than a single debit and credit. For example, assume that a piece of equipment, which cost $10,000, was sold. In exchange, $6,000 in cash and a $4,000 note were received. The journal entry, called a compound journal entry, would be:

Cash	6,000	
Note receivable	4,000	
Equipment		10,000

Questions:

1. What is a journal entry?
   a entry for a particular transaction (date, accounts, amounts)

2. What is a compound journal entry?
   transactions that include more than a single debit and credit

3. What is an account?
   a record of activity for a particular asset/equity

4. What is a ledger?
   a book holding account - an account record that are kept in financial statement order records for a co.

5. What are debits and credits?
   debits are entrys on the left side of an account. credits are on the right side. debits increase assets, and decrease equities. credits decrease assets and increase equities

6. What accounts normally carry a debit balance?
   assets, expenses, dividends

7. What accounts normally carry a credit balance?
   liabilities, cap stock, retained earnings, revenues

8. What is double-entry accounting?
   when the total of all debit entries are equal to the total of all credit entries.

Problems:

A. Journalize the following transactions.

1. Purchased merchandise on account for $65,000.
2. Made cash sales of $70,000.
3. Cost of goods sold in #2 was $42,000.
4. Spend $3,500 on miscellaneous expenses.
5. Paid salaries of $20,000.
6. Paid $30,000 on account.

B. Journalize the following transactions for the Smiling Onion Company (you may use whatever dates you choose – as long as they're all in the same year!):

1. Issued capital stock for cash of $90,000.
2. Purchased merchandise for $8,000 cash.
3. Made cash sales of $14,000.
4. The cost of the goods sold in #3 was $5,500.
5. Purchased merchandise on account for $80,000.
6. Spent $1,500 on advertising.
7. Sold merchandise on account for $110,000.
8. The cost of the goods sold in #7 was $60,000.
9. Paid rent of $7,500.
10. Paid salaries of $16,000.
11. Received payment from customers for $80,000.
12. Paid $20,000 in cash for land.
13. Salaries owed at the end of the year were $5,000.
14. Paid dividends of $2,500.

Test 1

This is a good time to check on your progress.

A. Record journal entries for the following transactions of Epitome Company for 2002.

Jan. 2 – Issued capital stock for cash, $60,000.
Jan. 6 – Purchased merchandise on account for $50,000.
Jan. 21 – Paid rent of $7,500.
Feb. 4 – Purchased land for cash, $10,000.
Feb. 10 – Sold merchandise for cash, $20,000. The cost of goods sold was $12,000.
Mar. 8 – Sold merchandise on account for $35,000. The cost of goods sold was $21,000.
Mar. 20 – Paid $50,000 on amount owed for inventory.
Apr. 15 – Received $35,000 from customers on account.
July 7 – Sold merchandise for cash, $25,000. The cost of goods sold was $15,000.
Aug. 12 – Purchased merchandise on account for $75,000.
Sept. 19 – Sold merchandise on account for $30,000. The cost of goods sold was $18,000.
Oct. 3 – Paid miscellaneous expenses of $5,000.
Oct. 15 – Received $20,000 on account from customers.
Nov. 1 – Paid $60,000 on amount owed for inventory.
Dec. 1 – Paid salaries of $20,000.
Dec. 31 – Paid dividends of $3,000.
Dec. 31 – Owed salaries of $1,500.

B. Prepare a transaction worksheet for the above transactions.

12000
21000
15000
18000

20000

85%

Everything should be made as simple as possible, but not one bit simpler.
~ Albert Einstein

Chart of Accounts

The Chart of Accounts is a listing of all of the accounts that a business has. When first setting up the accounting system for a business, you have to know what the business will do to help determine what kinds of accounts the business will need. This system can be very simple, such as would be used by a small sole proprietorship, or very complex, such as would be used by a large international corporation. The accounts are listed in financial statement order: assets, liabilities, the elements of owners' equity, revenues, and expenses. The numbering system should indicate classifications and relationships between the accounts. The number of digits depends on how much detail is required and the number of accounts the business needs. Generally there are no fewer than three digits.

Assuming a 4-digit account number is used, an explanation of the system follows.

$$X\ X\ X\ X$$
— Sub class
— Main sub class
— Main class

The first digit indicates a main classification.
1--- Assets and related contra accounts
2--- Liabilities
3--- Stockholders' equity
4--- Sales and related accounts
5--- Purchases and related accounts
6--- Operating expenses
7--- Other revenues and expenses
8--- Income Tax

The second digit indicates a main subclass.
11-- Current assets
12-- Long-term investments
13-- Property, plant, and equipment and related contra accounts
14-- Intangible assets
21-- Current liabilities
24-- Long-term liabilities

The third and fourth digits are further subclassifications and relationships.
2180 Withholding, Social Security, and Medicare tax payable
2181 Federal unemployment tax payable
2182 State unemployment tax payable

The third and fourth digits are often chosen for consistency or to show relationships. In the following example, the first digit denotes whether the account is an asset or liability; the second shows it is current; the final "30" that it is an account receivable or payable; and the "40" that it's a note receivable or payable.
1130 Accounts receivable
2130 Accounts payable

1140 Note receivable
2140 Note payable

Contra accounts, which are deducted from related accounts and will be discussed further in later chapters, can be shown with a final digit of "8" or "9".

> 1120 Accounts receivable
> 1129 Allowance for uncollectibles
> 1350 Computer equipment
> 1359 Accumulated depreciation – computer equipment
> 4000 Sales
> 4008 Sales returns and allowances
> 4009 Sales discounts

The following demonstrates numbers assigned to show relationships.

> 1181 Prepaid advertising
> 6081 Advertising expense
>
> 2160 Estimated income tax payable
> 8160 Income tax expense

Following is an example of a chart of accounts. Remember that this is not an exhaustive listing of all possible accounts. Depending on the business, there may be additional accounts and some of the accounts listed may not be included.

Current assets
1110 Cash
1120 Accounts receivable
1129 Allowance for uncollectibles
1130 Notes receivable
1145 Interest receivable
1160 Inventory
1181 Prepaid advertising
1182 Prepaid insurance
1183 Prepaid rent

Long-term investments
1210 Land
1220 Building
1230 Investments in bonds

Property, plant, and equipment
1310 Parking lot
1320 Store fixtures
1329 Accumulated depreciation – store fixtures
1340 Delivery equipment
1349 Accumulated depreciation – delivery equipment
1350 Computer equipment
1359 Accumulated depreciation – computer equipment

Intangible assets
1410 Patents
1420 Goodwill

Current liabilities
2120 Accounts payable
2130 Notes payable
2145 Interest payable
2155 Salaries payable
2160 Estimated income tax payable
2170 Liability for sales taxes
2180 Withholding, Social Security, and Medicare tax payable
2181 Federal unemployment tax payable
2182 State unemployment tax payable
2195 Advances from customers
2196 Rent received in advance

Long-term liabilities
2310 Mortgage payable

Stockholders' equity
3510 Capital stock
3511 Capital in excess of par value
3610 Retained earnings
3810 Dividends

Sales and related accounts
4000 Sales
4008 Sales returns and allowances
4009 Sales discounts

Purchases and related accounts
5170 Purchases
5178 Purchase returns and allowances
5179 Purchase discounts
5400 Cost of goods sold

Operating expenses
6001 Bad debts expense
6029 Depreciation expense – store fixtures
6049 Depreciation expense – delivery equipment
6059 Depreciation expense – computer equipment
6070 Miscellaneous selling expenses
6081 Advertising
6082 Insurance expense
6201 Office expenses
6255 Office salaries
6271 Other delivery expense
6301 Payroll taxes expense
6371 Salesmen's commissions
6383 Store rent
6411 Taxes, such as business and occupation taxes

Other revenues and gains
7010 Rent of land
7045 Interest revenue

Other expenses and losses
7145 Interest expense

Income tax
8160 Income tax

Exercises ~ 8

Questions:

1. What is a chart of accounts?

   a graph that shows a listing of all the accounts the business has.

2. In what order are the accounts listed?

   assets, liabilities, the elements of the owners equity, revenues and expenses

Problem:

Create a chart of accounts using four digits with the following accounts:

Cash
Accounts receivable
Interest receivable
Inventory
Prepaid advertising
Computer equipment
Accumulated depreciation
Accounts payable
Salaries payable
Advances from customers
Capital stock
Retained earnings
Dividends
Sales
Cost of goods sold
Depreciation expense
Advertising expense
Office expense
Rent expense
Salaries expense
Other expense

Whoso neglects learning in his youth,
loses the past and is dead for the future.
~ Euripides

Posting to the Ledger

Once the transactions are recorded in the journal, they need to be entered in the accounts in the ledger. This process is called posting. Using a T-account system, with the ledger account being debited shown on the left and the account being credited shown on the right and the number of the transaction corresponding to the entry in the T-account, we get the following results.

1. Issued capital stock for $40,000 cash.

Journal entry:

Cash	40,000	
Capital stock		40,000
Issued capital stock for cash		

Ledger entries:

Cash		Capital Stock	
1. 40,000			1. 40,000

2. Purchased equipment for $10,000 cash.

Journal entry:

Equipment	10,000	
Cash		10,000
Purchased equipment for cash		

Ledger entries:

Equipment		Cash	
2. 10,000		1. 40,000	2. 10,000

3. Purchased merchandise on account for $50,000.

Journal entry:

Merchandise	50,000	
Accounts payable		50,000
Purchased merchandise on account		

Ledger entries:

Merchandise		Accounts Payable	
3. 50,000			3. 50,000

While the above examples show clearly where debits and credits are recorded in the ledger accounts by using the T-account format, knowing the balance of the account is not as clear. In order to make it easier to know the balance while still keeping track of debits and credits, we will use a different form for the account. An example follows.

Account Title Cash   Account No. 111

			Ref.	Debit	Credit	Balance
2002						
Jan.	2	← This space is for explanation,		40,000		40,000 Dr.
	5	if needed →			10,000	30,000 Dr.

The posting process involves several steps. One transaction at a time is posted to the ledger. First, in the journal, enter the account number in the reference column to the left of the dollar amounts for each account in the transaction. Next, record the debit entry in the appropriate ledger account, including dollar amount in the debit column and the date. Then enter the page number of the journal that the transaction is on into the reference column to the left of the dollar amount in the ledger for that account. If an explanation for the entry is needed (usually it isn't), enter that into the explanation column. The credit entry would then be recorded in the appropriate ledger account in the same way that the debit entry was recorded, making sure you record the dollar amount in the credit column. If there is a beginning balance in an account (such as the ending balance from the previous year), it would be listed on the first line in the ledger.

Recording the account number in the reference column of the journal and the journal page number in the reference column of the ledger account helps in tracing the information between the two. This is important if there is an error that needs to be corrected. This process also helps to keep track of where you are in the posting process, in case you are interrupted before posting all of the transactions to the ledger accounts.

Below are the results of posting journal entries to the ledger. You should recognize these journal entries from Chapter 7.

Journal					Page 1	
2002						
Jan	2	Cash	111	27,000		
		Capital Stock	311		27,000	
		Issued capital stock for cash				
	5	Land	117	15,000		
		Cash	111		15,000	
		Purchased land for cash				
	10	Merchandise inventory	115	61,000		
		Accounts payable	211		61,000	
		Purchased inventory on account				
Feb	4	Accounts receivable	113	83,000		
		Revenue	411		83,000	
		Sales on account				
	4	Cost of goods sold	511	51,000		
		Merchandise inventory	115		51,000	
		Cost of goods sold				
Mar	1	Cash	111	73,500		
		Accounts receivable	113		73,500	
		Cash receipts from customers				
	15	Accounts payable	211	45,500		
		Cash	111		45,500	
		Payment on account				
May	15	Rent expense	515	6,000		
		Cash	111		6,000	
		Paid rent				
Oct	20	Miscellaneous expense	513	4,000		
		Cash	111		4,000	
		Paid miscellaneous expenses				
Dec	1	Salaries expense	517	14,500		
		Cash	111		14,500	
		Paid salaries				
	31	Salaries expense	517	3,000		
		Salaries payable	213		3,000	
		Unpaid salaries owed				
	31	Dividends	315	2,500		
		Cash	111		2,500	
		Paid dividends				

Ledger:

Account Title <u>Cash</u>   Account No. 111

2002			Ref	Debit	Credit	Balance
Jan.	2		1	27,000		27,000 Dr.
	5		1		15,000	12,000 Dr.
Mar.	1		1	73,500		85,500 Dr.
	15		1		45,500	40,000 Dr.
May	15		1		6,000	34,000 Dr.
Oct.	20		1		4,000	30,000 Dr.
Dec.	1		1		14,500	15,500 Dr.
	31		1		2,500	13,000 Dr.

Account Title <u>Accounts Receivable</u>   Account No. 113

2002			Ref	Debit	Credit	Balance
Feb.	4		1	83,000		83,000 Dr.
Mar.	1		1		73,500	9,500 Dr.

Account Title <u>Merchandise Inventory</u>   Account No. 115

2002			Ref	Debit	Credit	Balance
Jan.	10		1	61,000		61,000 Dr.
Feb.	4		1		51,000	10,000 Dr.

Account Title <u>Land</u>   Account No. 117

2002			Ref	Debit	Credit	Balance
Jan.	5		1	15,000		15,000 Dr.

Account Title <u>Accounts Payable</u>   Account No. 211

2002			Ref	Debit	Credit	Balance
Jan.	10		1		61,000	61,000 Cr.
Mar.	15		1	45,500		15,500 Cr.

Account Title <u>Salaries Payable</u>   Account No. 213

2002			Ref	Debit	Credit	Balance
Dec.	31		1		3,000	3,000 Cr.

Account Title <u>Capital Stock</u>   Account No. 311

2002			Ref	Debit	Credit	Balance
Jan.	2		1		27,000	27,000 Cr.

Account Title <u>Dividends</u>   Account No. 315

2002			Ref	Debit	Credit	Balance
Dec.	31		1	2,500		2,500 Dr.

Account Title Revenue   Account No. 411

		Ref	Debit	Credit	Balance
2002					
Feb.	4	1		83,000	83,000 Cr.

Account Title Cost of Goods Sold   Account No. 511

		Ref	Debit	Credit	Balance
2002					
Feb.	4	1	51,000		51,000 Dr.

Account Title Miscellaneous Expense   Account No. 513

		Ref	Debit	Credit	Balance
2002					
Oct.	20	1	4,000		4,000 Dr.

Account Title Rent Expense   Account No. 515

		Ref	Debit	Credit	Balance
2002					
May	15	1	6,000		6,000 Dr.

Account Title Salaries Expense   Account No. 517

		Ref	Debit	Credit	Balance
2002					
Dec.	1	1	14,500		14,500 Dr.
	31	1	3,000		17,500 Dr.

Since you have been using the double-entry method of accounting, in each of the transactions the debit entries have been equal to the credit entries. If you were to add up all of the debit entries and all of the credit entries from all of the transactions, the total debits would equal the total credits. Therefore, the total of all of the debit balances in the accounts will equal the total of all of the credit balances in the accounts.

Trial Balance

Periodically, the equality of the debit and credit balances in the ledger should be checked. This is done by listing and totaling all the account balances in the ledger. This listing of the account balances is called a trial balance. It is common practice to prepare a trial balance at the end of each month. The December 31, 2002 trial balance for ABC Supply Company, prepared after posting the 2002 journal entries, follows.

ABC Supply Company
Trial Balance
December 31, 2002

	Debit	Credit
Cash	13,000	
Accounts receivable	9,500	
Inventory	10,000	
Land	15,000	
Accounts payable		15,500
Salaries payable		3,000
Capital stock		27,000
Dividends	2,500	
Sales		83,000
Cost of Goods Sold	51,000	
Miscellaneous expense	4,000	
Rent expense	6,000	
Salaries expense	17,500	
	128,500	128,500

Note that retained earnings is not listed. Instead, its components of revenues and expenses are each listed separately. This is because the company began this year and there were no retained earnings from the previous year. Once this year's books have been closed, there will be a retained earnings account, which will appear on the trial balance for all future years. This will be discussed further in future chapters.

A trial balance is used to check the mathematical accuracy of the ledger. It will not tell you if a mistake has been made by posting to the wrong account or if a transaction wasn't posted to the ledger at all. It does allow you to know that you didn't leave out part of a journal entry when posting to the ledger, for example.

The trial balance can also be used in preparing periodic financial statements. All of the account balances are listed in one place from which to conveniently create the statements.

Exercises - 9

Questions:

1. What is posting? Describe the process.

I transaction at a time is posted to the ledger

2. Why don't we use the T-account format in the ledger?

there is an easier way

3. What is a trial balance?

its used to check the mathmatical accuracy of the ledger

4. How is the trial balance used?

in preparing periodic financial statements but it doesn't allow you to

Problems: *know that you didn't leave out part of the journal entry when posting*

A. Given the following journal entries, post the transactions to the ledger. The account numbers have already *to the ledger* been entered in the journal for you. The beginning balances in the accounts are as follows:

Cash - $25,000

Accounts receivable - $3,000

Inventory – $5,000

Accounts payable - $0

All revenue and expense accounts begin the month with a zero

1) in the jurnal, you enter the account no. in the Ref. column to the left of the dollar amount of each acc. in the transaction.

2) record the debit entry in the right ledger account + dollar amount in debit column + Date

3) enter the page no.

Journal

2003

Aug	1	Rent expense			
		Cash			
		Paid August rent			
	5	Inventory			
		Accounts payable			
		Purchased inventory on account			
	12	Accounts receivable *or Cash*			
		Sales			
		Sold merchandise on account *or for C*			
	12	Cost of goods sold	511	46,000	
		Inventory	115		46,000
		Cost of sales			
	20	Cash	111	69,000	
		Accounts receivable	113		69,000
		Received from customers			
	26	Accounts payable	211	80,000	
		Cash	111		80,000
		Paid on account			
	30	Salaries expense	519	4,500	
		Cash	111		4,500
		Paid salaries			

B. The chart of accounts and all transactions for Up 'N Down Corp. for the month of May, 2002 are listed below.

1. Journalize the transactions.
2. Post the transactions to the ledger accounts. (For conservation of paper, you may list more than one account on a page, if there is room.)
3. Prepare a trial balance.
4. Prepare the 2002 financial statements (balance sheet, statement of retained earnings, and income statement). Up 'N Down's fiscal year (year-long time period for tax and reporting purposes) ends May 31.

Chart of Accounts
111 Cash
113 Accounts receivable
115 Inventory
211 Accounts payable
213 Advertising payable
219 Salaries payable
311 Capital stock
315 Dividends
411 Sales
511 Cost of goods sold
513 Advertising expense
515 Office expense
517 Rent expense
519 Salaries expense

May 1 – The corporation was organized and 500 shares of stock were issued for cash in the amount of $5,000.

1 – A storefront was rented from the Real Estate Agency for $375 per month. The May rent was paid.

3 – Received on account 10 rubber dinghies from the Dinghy Company at an invoice price of $200 each.

5 – Paid Dinghy Company $1,500 on the account.

6 – Sales for the day were 3 dinghies. 2 were cash sales at $315 each and the third was sold on credit to A. Rower for $320.

9 – Paid balance owed to Dinghy Company and ordered 10 more dinghies.

11 – Paid $80 for newspaper advertising for the week ended May 4.

11 – Paid employees' wages for the week of $250.

12 – Sales for the day: Cash – 2 units @ $315 each
                         Credit – 2 units @ $320 each to John Fisher.

13 – Collected on accounts receivable $160.

15 – Received dinghies ordered on May 9 at an invoice price of $200 each. Payment is to be on account.

17 – Paid $80 for newspaper ad for week ending May 11.

18 – Paid employees' wages for week of $350.

20 – Sales for day: Cash – 5 units @ $315 each.
                     Credit – 1 unit @ $320 to Richard Slocumb
                              1 unit @ $320 to Charles Nogo
                              1 unit @ $320 to Harry Maxwell

21 – Collected $480 on account.

23 – Paid $80 for weekly newspaper ad.

24 – Paid Dinghy Company $1,500 on account.

25 – Paid employees' wages for week of $350.

26 – Purchased office supplies from Office Now for $100.

27 – Sales for day: Cash – 3 units @ 315.

29 – Received 10 dinghies from Dinghy Company at invoice price of $200 each. Payment is to be on account.

30 – Paid $80 for weekly newspaper ad. Additional advertising of $30 owed at end of month is to be paid next month.

31 – Owed wages of $300 that haven't been paid.

31 – Collected $320 on account.

31 – Paid dividends of $500.

Learn to listen. Opportunity could be knocking at your door very softly.
~ Frank Tyger

Income Determination

Determining the net income is important for a variety of reasons. It is an indication of debt-paying ability since profitable operations show that a company has the economic resources to pay its debts. (This may allow the company to receive a loan.) The production of net income also provides the resources to maintain existing operations, or even expand them. As stated earlier, net income is the excess of revenues over expenses for a given period of time. Conversely, a net loss is the excess of expenses over revenues. Thus, net income is the dollar amount by which the company has become economically better off during the period of time being reported on. Net income increases the company's assets and retained earnings.

Businesses engage in economic operations in order to produce income. The primary ongoing economic activities or processes in which the business is engaged are the operations of the business. These operations can be buying and selling products (a retailing company), manufacturing and selling the products produced (a manufacturing company), or selling services (a service company). The business uses economic inputs (resources) to provide outputs (goods and services) to its customers. The assets received from customers for the company's goods and services for a specific time period are revenues. The cost of the resources used to provide those goods and services for the same time period are expenses. The excess of revenues produced from operations over operating expenses during a specific time period is net operating income.

A business also can have economic activities not directly tied to its normal operations (its primary income generating activities). These secondary activities result in nonoperating revenues and/or expenses. Some nonoperating revenues are interest, dividend, and rent revenues. A nonoperating expense would be interest expense. An example of a gain or loss would be the gain or loss from selling land or equipment used in the business that is not held for sale in the regular operations of the company. Since nonoperating revenues and expenses do have an effect on retained earnings, and thus on stockholders' equity, they are included in the determination of net income. However, since the primary determination of net income comes from the operations of the business, net income is often referred to as the results of operations. Some companies go a step further and separate operating revenues and expenses from nonoperating revenues and expenses on the income statement as shown below.

Big Company
Income Statement
For the Year Ended December 31, 20XX

Revenues from operations		$X,XXX
Expenses from operations		(XXX)
Net operating income		$XXX
Nonoperating revenues	$XXX	
Nonoperating expenses	(XX)	XX
Net income		$XXX

Keep in mind that a company's net income is not the same as its net cash inflow. Net income is determined by revenues and expenses rather than cash receipts and expenditures. This will be discussed in more detail later.

Periodic Financial Statements

The time period used by accountants and bookkeepers for financial statement reporting is called the accounting, or fiscal, period. This is the time period covered by the income statement. The income statement, statement of retained earnings, and statement of cash flow cover a specific fiscal period, while the balance sheet is as of a specific date at the end of the fiscal period.

Normally, the accounting period is twelve consecutive months, referred to as the fiscal year. For most businesses, the fiscal year is the calendar year ending on December 31. Some companies may base their fiscal year on their yearly business cycle. An automobile manufacturer could end its fiscal year in late summer, just before introducing the new model year so that its fiscal year and its car model year are the same. Department stores often end their fiscal year on January 31 after their peak season and the clearance sales in January. The federal government ends its fiscal year on September 30.

Those in management of many businesses want to see financial statements produced every month (some even more often) in order to keep track of where the company is financially and operationally. This allows them to plan more efficiently and to respond more quickly to what is happening with the business. Publicly owned businesses (such as some corporations) prepare and distribute financial reports quarterly to the Securities and Exchange Commission (SEC), the stock exchange where their stock is listed, and to their shareholders. Monthly, quarterly, or semiannual financial statements are interim statements, as opposed to the annual statements issued at the end of the fiscal year.

Fiscal Period Assumption - chapter 4 of AG

In order to prepare periodic financial statements, the assumption is made that the economic activity of the business stops at these periodic intervals. This is called the Fiscal Period Assumption. It is assumed that the business activity stops to allow the accountant to prepare financial statements and to thus report on the company's progress and change in financial position during the period just ended and its financial position at the end of the period. This, in effect, is really just an estimate of where the company is. The exact results of the company's business activities can't accurately be determined until the business operations have been discontinued.

Even though the Fiscal Period Assumption has business activity stopping briefly at a particular point in time, in reality, some business transactions cross over between two, or even more, accounting periods. In order to avoid the distortion this can cause, there has to be a cut-off between periods. There are two assumptions that are used to avoid this distortion: the Revenue Recognition Assumption and the Matching Assumption. These will be explained in the following paragraphs. The application of these two assumptions gives us the accrual basis of accounting. The accrual basis of accounting recognizes revenue during the period it is earned and recognizes expenses during the period they are incurred in generating that revenue, regardless of cash flow.

Revenue Recognition Assumption

The Revenue Recognition Assumption states that revenue is recognized in the period in which it is earned. Determining exactly when revenue has been earned can be difficult. It could be when orders are received from customers, when the manufacturing process is completed, when goods are delivered to the customer, or when payment is received. Generally, for retail, wholesale, and manufacturing businesses, the point (date) of sale is used for revenue recognition. There are three reasons for this:

1. By the time the point of sale has been reached, the bulk of the economic effort needed to generate revenue has already been performed.
2. The exchange price at the point of sale gives an objective measurement of revenue.
3. A conversion takes place at the point of sale – an exchange of one asset for another.

For service-type businesses, revenue is recognized when the service is performed. In those situations where the performance of the service covers more than one accounting period, estimates often can be made as to how much revenue has been earned in each period.

Matching Assumption

The Matching Assumption states that expenses used to generate revenue should be matched with that revenue when it is earned. This matching assumes that there is a direct relationship between expenses and revenues. Often that is true. However, in some cases there is no direct connection between the two. There are, therefore, two ways of associating expenses with revenue.

The first way of associating expenses with revenues is direct association. Expenses are directly related to revenue if they are for goods and services used to produce the company's product (whether goods or services). The cost of these goods and services are expensed when the revenue is earned through the sales of the company. An example is the expensing of the cost of goods sold for a manufacturing company when those goods are sold. Sales commissions are another direct expenses since the sales commissions wouldn't exist without a sale being made.

The second way of associating expenses with revenues is indirect association. Expenses that cannot be directly connected to the production of a company's product are indirect expenses. The cost of these goods and services are expensed during the period in which they are incurred. They are associated with a period rather than revenues. Examples of period expenses include administrative salaries, insurance, taxes, and advertising. These are the operating expenses.

As just stated, cost is how we measure expense. It is also the measure for acquiring assets. The cost of an asset is its purchase price plus any related additional outlays (incidental costs such as legal fees and shipping charges). If, at the time of a cost outlay, it is known that the associated economic benefit will not last beyond the current operating period, the transaction is generally recorded as an expense. An example of this would be paying for a year's worth of advertising in a magazine at the beginning of the year. The same result, but with more work, can be achieved by recording the cost as an asset (prepaid expense) at the beginning of the year and transferring the amount to an expense account when the benefit is expired or consumed. If the management of the company is concerned with tracking expenses month by month, the second method is more appropriate since it shows which month, or months, the benefit was realized and expensed. (chapter 4)

If, on the other hand, it is expected that a cost outlay will have economic benefit beyond the current accounting period, the transaction is generally recorded as an asset acquisition. An example of this would be the purchase of manufacturing equipment. In each accounting period, as benefits expire or are consumed, an appropriate amount is transferred to an expense account.

The second year of operations of ABC Supply Company will be used to continue the understanding of accrual accounting. A journal entry will be shown and T-accounts will be used to review the use of debits and credits. Transactions that occur repeatedly will be combined, such as salary payments and purchasing inventory. The number of the transaction will be used for the corresponding entry in the T-account. Accounts being debited will be shown on the left; accounts being credited will be on the right.

2003 Transactions:
1. Paid the liability for December 2002 salaries, $3,000.

   Explanation: Salaries are an expense that apply to the period in which the employees performed the services. The payment of the salaries doesn't always occur in the same period that the work was performed. These salaries were recorded as expense in December 2002 because that was when the work was performed and a liability was created. The payment in 2003 removes the outstanding liability.

| Salaries payable (Liability) | decrease | 3,000 | |
| Cash (Asset) | decrease | | 3,000 |

Salaries Payable			Cash		
1.	3,000	1/1/03 balance 3,000	1/1/03 balance 13,000	1.	3,000

2. Purchased merchandise on account, $75,000.

| Inventory (Asset) | increase | 75,000 | |
| Accounts payable (Liability) | increase | | 75,000 |

Inventory			Accounts Payable		
1/1/03 balance	10,000			1/1/03 balance	15,500
2.	75,000			2.	75,000

3. Purchased a delivery truck for cash, $6,000. Management believes it will last for six years.

   Explanation: Acquiring the truck has secured future economic benefit for the company. Since the benefit will last beyond the current period, the transaction is recorded as an asset acquisition.

| Delivery truck (Asset) | increase | 6,000 | |
| Cash (Asset) | decrease | | 6,000 |

Delivery Truck			Cash		
1/1/03 balance	0		1/1/03 balance	13,000	1. 3,000
3.	6,000				3. 6,000

4a. Sales on account, $118,000.

Accounts receivable (Asset)	increase	118,000	
Sales (Revenue)	increase		118,000

Accounts Receivable				Sales			
1/1/03 balance	9,500					**4a.**	118,000
4a.	118,000						

4b. Cost of goods sold, $70,000.

Cost of goods sold (Expense)	increase	70,000	
Inventory (Asset)	decrease		70,000

Cost of Goods Sold				Inventory			
4b.	70,000			1/1/03 balance	10,000	**4b.**	70,000
				2.	75,000		

5. Collections from customers $123,000.

Cash (Asset)	increase	123,000	
Accounts receivable (Asset)	decrease		123,000

Cash				Accounts Receivable			
1/1/03 balance	13,000	1.	3,000	1/1/03 balance	9,500	**5.**	123,000
5.	123,000	3.	6,000	4a.	118,000		

6. Payment to creditors, $65,000.

Accounts payable (Liability)	decrease	65,000	
Cash (Asset)	decrease		65,000

Accounts Payable				Cash			
6.	65,000	1/1/03 balance	15,500	1/1/03 balance	13,000	1.	3,000
		2.	75,000	5.	123,000	3.	6,000
						6.	65,000

7. Paid three years' rent in advance, $18,000.

Explanation: The company has acquired the right to the future economic benefits of having the use of the rented property beyond the current period. Therefore, this qualifies as an asset acquisition.

Prepaid rent (Asset)	increase	18,000	
Cash (Asset)	decrease		18,000

Prepaid Rent				Cash			
7.	18,000			1/1/03 balance	13,000	1.	3,000
				5.	123,000	3.	6,000
						6.	65,000
						7.	18,000

8. On September 1, 2003, $12,000 was invested in 10% bonds. The bonds specify that interest will be paid semiannually on March 1 and September 1.

Explanation: An asset, bond investment, was acquired at a cost of $12,000 in order to earn interest revenue.

Bond investment (Asset)	increase	12,000	
Cash (Asset)	decrease		12,000

Bond Investment				Cash			
8.	12,000			1/1/03 balance	13,000	1.	3,000
				5.	123,000	3.	6,000
						6.	65,000
						7.	18,000
						8.	12,000

9. Paid other expenses, $2,500.

Other expenses (Expense)	increase	2,500	
Cash (Asset)	decrease		2,500

Other Expenses			Cash			
9.	2,500	1/1/03 balance	13,000	1.		3,000
		5.	123,000	3.		6,000
				6.		65,000
				7.		18,000
				8.		12,000
				9.		2,500

10. Received $4,000 cash from customers for special order merchandise in advance. The two units, each to sell for $2,000, have been ordered by ABC Supply Company. One unit will be received in December and the other in February of next year.

> Explanation: Since the items ordered haven't been delivered to the customer, the $4,000 can't be recorded as revenue. The company has an obligation to its customer to deliver the merchandise. Until that occurs, the company has a liability called Advances from Customers.

Cash (Asset)	increase	4,000	
Advances from customers (Liability)	increase		4,000

Cash				Advances from Customers		
1/1/03 balance	13,000	1.	3,000		10.	4,000
5.	123,000	3.	6,000			
10.	4,000	6.	65,000			
		7.	18,000			
		8.	12,000			
		9.	2,500			

11. Paid salaries for January through November 2003, $27,000.

Salaries expense (Expense)	increase	27,000	
Cash (Asset)	decrease		27,000

Salaries Expense			Cash			
11.	27,000	1/1/03 balance	13,000	1.		3,000
		5.	123,000	3.		6,000
		10.	4,000	6.		65,000
				7.		18,000
				8.		12,000
				9.		2,500
				11.		27,000

12. Dividends were authorized to be paid by the board of directors in the amount of $2,000.

Dividends (Dividend)	increase	2,000	
Cash (Asset)	decrease		2,000

Dividends			Cash			
12.	2,000	1/1/03 balance	13,000	1.		3,000
		5.	123,000	3.		6,000
		10.	4,000	6.		65,000
				7.		18,000
				8.		12,000
				9.		2,500
				11.		27,000
				12.		2,000

13. Received the first of the two special-ordered units. The cost was $1,200 and the sales price was $2,000.

| Merchandise inventory (Asset) | increase | 1,200 | |
| Cash (Asset) | decrease | | 1,200 |

Merchandise Inventory					Cash			
1/1/03 balance	10,000	4b.	70,000	1/1/03 balance	13,000	1.	3,000
2.	75,000			5.	123,000	3.	6,000
13.	1,200			10.	4,000	6.	65,000
						7.	18,000
						8.	12,000
						9.	2,500
						11.	27,000
						12.	2,000
						13.	1,200

The results of the above transactions are summarized in the following trial balance by adding and subtracting the amounts in the T-accounts to determine the ending balance. It is labeled as an unadjusted trial balance because there are some adjustments that need to be made to properly match revenues and expenses for the current period. These adjusting entries will be explained in the next chapter.

ABC Supply Company
Unadjusted Trial Balance
December 31, 2003

Cash	3,300	
Account receivable	4,500	
Merchandise Inventory	16,200	
Prepaid rent	18,000	
Bond investment	12,000	
Delivery truck	6,000	
Land	15,000	
Accounts payable		25,500
Advances from customers		4,000
Capital stock		27,000
Retained earnings		2,000
Dividends	2,000	
Sales		118,000
Cost of goods sold	70,000	
Salaries expense	27,000	
Other expenses	2,500	
	176,500	176,500

Note that there is an entry for retained earnings. This is because it is the second year of operations of ABC Supply Company. At the end of 2002, all of the revenue and expense accounts were closed and balances transferred to retained earnings. This balance is carried forward in the retained earnings general ledger account. This process will be discussed in a future chapter.

Questions:

1. What is net income?

2. What are revenues?

3. What are expenses?

4. What are nonoperating revenues and expenses?

5. What is an accounting, or fiscal, period?

6. What is the Fiscal Period Assumption?

7. What is the Revenue Recognition Assumption?

8. What is the Matching Assumption?

9. What is the accrual basis of accounting?

10. What are the two ways of associating expenses with revenue?

11. How do you determine whether a cost outlay should be recorded as an expense or an asset?

Problems:

A. Record journal entries in a journal for the following transactions.

1. Purchased equipment for $7,500 on account. It is expected to have a useful life of 3 years.
2. Paid salaries of $4,800. Work was performed in the previous period.
3. Received $2,500 from a customer for a non-stocked item. The item is ordered and will be received next month.
4. Paid miscellaneous expenses of $1,600.
5. Purchased 6% bonds for $6,000 cash.

B. Given the following information, *Pg 44 + 45*
1. Journalize the transaction (don't worry about specific dates – this is combined information for the year).
2. Post transactions to the ledger. Make sure you record the beginning balances from the balance sheet (each year's ending balance is the next year's beginning balance).
3. Prepare an unadjusted trial balance for 2005.

Speed Corporation sells bicycles. Their Chart of Accounts and 2004 balance sheet is as follows:

Chart of Accounts
111   Cash
113   Accounts receivable
115   Inventory
121   Bond investment
131   Land
133   Building
134   Accumulated depreciation
211   Accounts payable
219   Salaries payable
311   Capital stock
313   Retained earnings
315   Dividends
411   Sales
511   Cost of goods sold
515   Other expense
519   Salaries expense
534   Depreciation expense

Speed Corporation
Balance Sheet
December 31, 2004

Assets:
Current assets:
Cash		$9,500	
Accounts receivable		37,000	
Inventory		45,000	$91,500

Property, plant, and equipment:
Land		$10,000	
Building	$165,500		
Accumulated depreciation	3,500	162,000	172,000
			$263,500

Equities
Current liabilities:
Accounts payable		$5,500	
Salaries payable		2,000	$7,500

Stockholders' equity:
Capital stock (1,000 shares)		$200,000	
Retained earnings		56,000	256,000
			$263,500

2005 transactions:

1. Received $33,500 from customers on account.

2. Paid December 2004 salaries owed of $2,000.

3a. Made cash sales of $43,000.

3b. The cost of the sales was $27,000.

4. Purchased $45,000 worth of merchandise on account.

5. Made an investment in bonds (a long-term asset) of $7,500.

6. Paid $26,000 on amount owed for inventory.

7a. Made sales on account in the amount of $78,000.

7b. Cost of sales was $51,000.

8. Paid other expenses of $2,400.

9. Paid salaries for January through November 2005 of $28,000.

10. The Board of Directors authorized the payment of dividends in the amount of $2,500.

Always do what you are afraid to do.
~ Ralph Waldo Emerson

Adjusting Entries

In the previous chapter, we prepared an unadjusted trial balance. It is referred to as such because some adjustments need to be made to the year-end balances in order to have them accurately reflect the activities of the year; to properly match revenues and expenses. Adjusting entries fall into the following groups:

1. Unrecorded revenues, often called accrued revenue.
2. Unrecorded expenses, often called accrued expense.
3. Earned advances from customers.
4. Cost expirations.

In this chapter, we are going to continue working with ABC Supply Company's books. In the examples, when an adjusting entry affects an account that had transactions recorded in it in Chapter 10, you will see those transactions again in the T-accounts. The necessary end-of-period adjustments for ABC Supply Company fall into the following categories.

A. Recognition of depreciation on the delivery truck. We depreciate assets that can be used up, wear out, decay, or become obsolete over their useful life. This is a recognition of the reduction of the value of the long-term asset over time.

B. Recognition of December salaries. Since the company records and pays salaries on the first business day of the following month, December salaries have not yet been recorded.

C. Recognition of one-third of the rent paid in advance as an expense for 2003.

D. Recognition of interest revenue earned on the bond investment. Even though no interest will be paid until March, interest is earned for the four months the bonds have been held.

E. Recognition of the portion of cash advances that have become earned. One special-ordered unit was received and delivered to the customer with a sales price of $2,000. This needs to be recognized as revenue.

Following is the process for recording the above adjusting entries.

A. Depreciation, the cost of the benefit received from using the truck, must be expensed. There are multiple methods of computing depreciation, the simplest of which is to assume an equal amount of the asset's cost should be assigned to each year's operations. This is called straight-line depreciation and is determined as follows:

Cost of asset	$6,000
Deduct estimated salvage (amount expected to be received when asset is disposed of)	600
Amount subject to depreciation	$5,400
Useful life – 6 years	
Annual depreciation ($5,400 ÷ 6)	$900

Explanation: Recognizing the services provided from the use of the truck by expensing depreciation properly matches expenses with generation of income for the period. Depreciation is not a cash expense, since no cash is being paid out over time. Since the asset is used over time, its cost is expensed over time according to accrual accounting. Instead of showing the undepreciated amount on the balance sheet, we use a contra asset account, accumulated depreciation. This allows the cost of the asset to remain on the balance sheet with the amount depreciated shown separately. Accumulated depreciation is a contra asset account because it is a deduction from an asset account.

| Depreciation expense (Expense) | increase | 900 | |
| Accumulated depreciation (Contra Asset) | increase | | 900 |

Depreciation Expense		Accumulated Depreciation		
A.	900		1/1/03 balance	0
			A.	900

B. December salaries owed of $2,500 must be recorded.

> Explanation: The work has been performed, therefore it is a liability owed by the company.

| Salaries expense (Expense) | increase | 2,500 | |
| Salaries payable (Liability) | increase | | 2,500 |

Salaries Expense		Salaries Payable		
11.	27,000	1.	3,000	1/1/03 balance 3,000
B.	2,500			B. 2,500

C. One-third of the rent paid in advance must be recognized as expense. $18,000 was paid at the beginning of 2003, so the annual rent is $6,000.

| Rent expense (Expense) | increase | 6,000 | |
| Prepaid rent (Asset) | decrease | | 6,000 |

Rent Expense		Prepaid Rent		
C.	6,000	7.	18,000	C. 6,000

D. Record interest revenue earned on bond investment for the four months since September 1. The interest is determined as follows:

Interest = Amount invested x Rate of interest x Period of time
$400 = $12,000 x 0.10 x 4/12

> Explanation: Because of accrual accounting, revenues must be recorded in the time period earned, regardless of cash flow. The interest on the bond is earned continually; cash payment is made twice a year.

| Interest receivable (Asset) | increase | 400 | |
| Interest revenue (Revenue) | increase | | 400 |

Interest Receivable		Interest Revenue	
D.	400	D.	400

E. Record sales revenue of $2,000 and reduction of liability from special-ordered unit received in December. Also, the cost of the unit sold, in the amount of $1,200, and the corresponding reduction in inventory needs to be recorded in the usual manner.

> Explanation: Once the unit was delivered to the customer, the obligation of the company to deliver is satisfied and the revenue has been earned.

Advances from customers (Liability)	decrease	2,000	
Sales (Revenue)	increase		2,000
Cost of goods sold (Expense)	increase	1,200	
Inventory (Asset)	decrease		1,200

Advances from Customers				Sales		
E.	2,000	10.	4,000		4a.	118,000
					E.	2,000

Cost of Goods Sold		Inventory			
4b.	70,000	1/1/03 balance	10,000	4b.	70,000
E.	1,200	2.	75,000	E.	1,200
		13.	1,200		

Once the adjusting entries have been journalized and posted, an adjusted trial balance is prepared. This allows us to be sure that the ledger is still in balance. It also is a convenient place from which to draw the information for preparing the financial statements. The adjusted trial balance for ABC Supply Company is below. Note that the only changes that have taken place are from the adjustments we have just made.

ABC Supply Company
Adjusted Trial Balance
December 31, 2003

Cash	3,300	
Accounts receivable	4,500	
Interest receivable	400	
Inventory	15,000	
Prepaid rent	12,000	
Bond investment	12,000	
Delivery truck	6,000	
Accumulated depreciation		900
Land	15,000	
Accounts payable		25,500
Advances from customers		2,000
Salaries payable		2,500
Capital stock		27,000
Retained earnings		2,000
Dividends	2,000	
Sales		120,000
Cost of goods sold	71,200	
Salaries expense	29,500	
Rent expense	6,000	
Other expense	2,500	
Depreciation expense	900	
Interest revenue		400
	180,300	180,300

We can now prepare the income statement. Sometimes we may wish to compare the current year to the previous year. When that is the case, a comparative income statement can be prepared as shown in the next example.

ABC Supply Company
Income Statement
For the Years Ended December 31, 2003 and 2002

	2003		2002	
Revenues:				
Sales	$120,000		$83,000	
Interest	400	$120,400		$83,000
Expenses:				
Cost of goods sold	$71,200		$51,000	
Other expense	2,500		4,000	
Rent expense	6,000		6,000	
Salaries expense	29,500		17,500	
Depreciation expense	900	110,100		78,500
Net income		$10,300		$4,500
Earnings per share (2,700 shares)		$3.81		$1.67

This example demonstrates an income statement in single-step format. All revenues are grouped together, all expenses are grouped together, and then in one step the expenses are subtracted from the revenues to arrive at net income.

In the multi-step format, we show groups of data and report an income figure for each group before arriving at net income. Each intermediate income amount is a "step" in the process. This multi-step format is illustrated below.

ABC Supply Company
Income Statement
For the Years Ended December 31, 2003 and 2002

		2003			2002	
Sales			$120,000			$83,000
Cost of goods sold			71,200			51,000
Gross margin			$48,800			$32,000
Operating expenses:						
Selling expenses:						
Sales salaries	$23,000			$14,000		
Depreciation	900	$23,900			$14,000	
General & administrative expenses:						
Salaries	$6,500			$3,500		
Rent	6,000			6,000		
Other	2,500	15,000		4,000	13,500	
Total operating expenses			38,900			27,500
Net operating income			$9,900			$4,500
Nonoperating items:						
Add: Interest revenue			400			
Net income			$10,300			$4,500
Earnings per share (2,700 shares)			$3.81			$1.67

The first intermediate income amount in the above income statement is for gross margin. This provides information on the amount of markup on the cost of the goods sold, on average, for the company. For ABC Supply Company, the average markup for 2003 is 41% (48,800 divided by 120,000) and for 2002 is 39% (32,000 divided by 83,000). The second interim step, net operating income, shows income from normal, recurring, and primary activities of the business.

By dividing the data into groups in the multi-step format, we also show expenses by their classifications: cost of goods sold, selling expenses, and general and administrative expenses. Cost of goods sold is the expense associated with the product purchased or produced that was sold during this period. Selling expenses are those expenses directly related to the effort put into promoting and selling the product of the company. General and administrative expenses are the costs of running the company.

Nonoperating Items

Nonoperating items are the revenues and expenses that are not directly related to the primary operations of the company. These would include interest earned on investments or the gain realized on the sale of a capital asset (an asset that is not what the company is in business to sell, e.g., a delivery truck). Nonoperating expenses would include items such as interest paid as a result of borrowing money or a loss from the sale of a capital asset.

Since nonoperating items are not part of the primary operations of the business, they are reported net on the income statement. When an item is reported net, only the gain or loss is reported, i.e., receipts minus costs. For example, this means that we don't report the amount of the sale of land held for investment and its original cost the way we show sales separate from the cost of goods sold. Instead, we just report the actual amount of the gain or loss (sales amount minus original cost). In a single-step format, nonoperating items are reported as separate line items with either revenues or expenses, whichever is appropriate. In a multi-step format, they are together under a separate heading, such as "Nonoperating items."

Extraordinary Items

Occasionally, there will be a gain or loss from an event that is unusual and infrequent for the business. These items would be reported as extraordinary gains or losses. Examples of extraordinary items would include losses from flood or tornado damage that are rare in the area, or the effects of a newly enacted law. Below is an example of an extraordinary item on a partial income statement. Assume that there were 8,000 shares of stock outstanding. Note that earnings per share is shown before the effect of the extraordinary item and net of it.

Income before extraordinary items	$60,000
Extraordinary item:	
Loss from earthquake damage	(4,000)
Net income	$56,000
Earnings per share:	
Income before extraordinary items	$7.50
Extraordinary loss	(0.50)
Net income	$7.00

Exercises – 11

Questions:

1. What are adjusting entries? *made at the end of the year to adjust account balances to acurateely reflect th activity of the year.*

unrecorded revenues/accrued revenue. unrecorded expenses/accrued expense.

2. What is depreciation? *earned advances from customers, and cost expirations*
depreciation decrease th value of an asset over three

3. What is a single-step format income statement?

4. What is a multi-step format income statement?

5. What are selling expenses?

6. What are general and administrative expenses?

7. What are nonoperating revenues and expenses?

8. How are nonoperating items reported on the income statement?

9. What is an extraordinary item?

Marinelli

Marinelli

Problems:

A. Journalize the following adjusting entries for Speed Corporation for 2005.

1. Record December salaries of $2,600, to be paid in January, 2006.
2. Record accrued interest on bond investment. $7,500 was invested August 1 at 5% interest to be paid February 1 and August 1.
3. Recognize as expense the used portion of prepaid advertising. One year of advertising was paid for on July 1 for $2,400.

B. Given the following information,
1. Journalize the adjusting entries for We Try Harder, Inc.
2. Post the transactions to the ledger. Use the amounts from the unadjusted trial balance for the beginning balances in order to arrive at the correct final totals.
3. Prepare an adjusted trial balance for 2005.
4. Prepare a multi-step income statement for 2005. The sales salaries are $24,000. There are 9,000 shares of stock issued.

Chart of Accounts

111   Cash
113   Accounts receivable
115   Interest receivable
117   Inventory
121   Prepaid insurance
123   Bond investment
133   Delivery van
134   Accumulated depreciation
211   Accounts payable
219   Salaries payable
311   Capital stock
313   Retained earnings
315   Dividends
411   Sales

Chart of Accounts continued

413 Interest income
511 Cost of goods sold
515 Other expense
519 Salaries expense
521 Insurance expense
534 Depreciation expense

We Try Harder, Inc.
Unadjusted Trial Balance
December 31, 2005

Cash	21,000	
Accounts receivable	60,000	
Inventory	19,000	
Prepaid insurance	3,000	
Bond investment	10,000	
Delivery van	16,000	
Accounts payable		30,000
Salaries payable		0
Capital stock		63,000
Retained earnings		22,000
Dividends	2,000	
Sales		135,000
Cost of goods sold	81,000	
Other expense	5,000	
Salaries expense	33,000	
	250,000	250,000

Adjustments:
1. Record salaries for December of $3,000, to be paid in January, 2006.
2. Record interest earned on bond investment. The bonds were purchased on October 1, 2005 for $10,000 at 6% interest. The interest is to be paid annually on October 1.
3. Record depreciation expense on delivery van. The van was purchased for $16,000 with a $1,000 salvage value. It is expected to have a 5-year life.
4. A two-year insurance policy was purchased at the beginning of the year for $3,000. The portion of the insurance premium applying to this year needs to be recognized as expense.

A pessimist sees the difficulty in every opportunity;
an optimist sees the opportunity in every difficulty.
~ Winston Churchill

Closing Entries

We are not yet finished making entries. Once the adjusting entries are posted to the ledger and the financial statements have been produced, we need to make some closing entries. Closing entries are those journal entries made to reduce temporary accounts to zero. Temporary accounts are revenue, expense, gain, and loss accounts. These are the accounts which are used to produce the income statement. Remember that revenue amounts increase retained earnings and expense amounts decrease retained earnings. This is seen when we add net income to retained earnings on the retained earnings statement. Since we want to see what net income is for the current fiscal period only, we need the revenue and expense accounts to start out with a zero balance at the beginning of the period. This is accomplished by the closing entries being journalized and posted, thereby closing the accounts. In contrast to the temporary accounts of revenues and expenses, accounts such as retained earnings in which the balance is carried forward from year to year are called permanent, or real, accounts.

Closing entries are made at the end of the year. They are journalized and then posted immediately after. Once the accounts are closed for a fiscal year, no more adjustments can be made to them; that year is closed. Since revenue and gain accounts normally carry credit balances, they are closed by making a debit entry for the balance. Expense and loss accounts normally carry a debit balance, so they are closed with a credit entry in the amount of the account balance. The difference between the debit and credit entries result in a credit to retained earnings for net income or a debit to retained earnings for a net loss. The dividends account is also a temporary account, but since it is not part of net income (it's not an expense account) it is closed with a separate entry from revenues and expenses.

Let's look again at ABC Supply Company. Here is the balance sheet for December 31, 2002.

ABC Supply Company
Balance Sheet
December 31, 2002

Assets			Equities		
Current assets:			Current liabilities:		
Cash	$13,000		Accounts Payable	$15,500	
Accounts Receivable	9,500		Salaries Payable	3,000	$18,500
Inventory	10,000	$32,500			
			Stockholders' equity:		
Long-term investment:			Capital stock, 2,700 shares		
Investment in land		15,000	issued & outstanding	$27,000	
		$47,500	Retained earnings	2,000	29,000
					$47,500

Notice that there is an amount for retained earnings of $2,000. Now let's look again at the trial balance for the same time period.

ABC Supply Company
Trial Balance
December 31, 2002

	Debit	Credit
Cash	13,000	
Accounts receivable	9,500	
Inventory	10,000	
Land	15,000	
Accounts payable		15,500
Salaries payable		3,000
Capital stock		27,000
Dividends	2,500	
Sales		83,000
Cost of Goods Sold	51,000	
Miscellaneous expense	4,000	
Rent expense	6,000	
Salaries expense	17,500	
	128,500	128,500

2000 (handwritten)

Notice here that there is no amount listed for retained earnings. Since ABC Supply Company was started at the beginning of 2002, there was no balance in the retained earnings account to bring forward. When the trial balance was created, the retained earnings account balance was still zero. The amounts that make up the $2,000 retained earnings amount are found in the revenue, expense, and dividend accounts.

Retained Earnings Balance

Let's summarize all the accounts which make up the retained earnings balance for 2002.

Revenue:
Sales – this has a credit balance		$83,000

Expense:
Cost of goods sold	$51,000	
Miscellaneous expense	4,000	
Rent expense	6,000	
Salaries expense	17,500	
These have a debit balance		78,500
Net income – a net credit		$4,500
Dividends – a debit balance		2,500
The difference (a net credit) is retained earnings		$2,000

These amounts are transferred to the retained earnings account through the following journal entries, the closing entries.

Journal					Page X	
2002						
Dec	31	Sales	411	83,000		
		Cost of goods sold	511		51,000	
		Miscellaneous expense	513		4,000	
		Rent expense	515		6,000	
		Salaries expense	517		17,500	
		Retained earnings	313		4,500	→ balancing figure
		To close revenue and expense				
		accounts and transfer net income				
		to retained earnings				
	31	Retained earnings	313	2,500		
		Dividends	315		2,500	
		To close dividend account and				
		transfer dividends to retained				
		earnings				

The closing entries are posted to the ledger as follows. I am just showing you the retained earnings and dividend accounts; the revenue and expense accounts would be done in the same way as the dividend account.

Account Title   Retained Earnings   Account No. 313

2002			Ref.	Debit	Credit	Balance
Dec	31		X		4,500	4,500 Cr.
	31		X	2,500		2,000 Cr.

Account Title   Dividends   Account No. 315

2002			Ref.	Debit	Credit	Balance
Dec	31	Year-end bal before closing				2,500 Dr.
	31		X		2,500	0 Dr.

After the books are closed, an after-closing, or post-closing, trial balance should be prepared to make sure that the debits and credits are still equal.

ABC Supply Company
Post-Closing Trial Balance
December 31, 2002

	Debit	Credit
Cash	13,000	
Accounts receivable	9,500	
Inventory	10,000	
Land	15,000	
Accounts payable		15,500
Salaries payable		3,000
Capital stock		27,000
Retained earnings		2,000
	47,500	47,500

Notice that only asset and equity accounts appear on this trial balance since the temporary accounts have been closed.

Financial Statement Worksheets

Sometimes a worksheet is used to aid in preparing the end-of-period adjusting entries, financial statements, and closing entries. This puts everything in one place to reduce the possibility of errors. If an accounting software program is being used, this would not be necessary. Also, in the case of a company that has few accounts in the ledger and few adjusting entries, a financial statement worksheet would not be necessary. It is when there are many accounts and/or adjusting entries in a manual system that the worksheet is the most useful.

Here are the steps for preparing a financial statement worksheet. On the following page is a prepared worksheet for ABC Supply Company for the year ended December 31, 2003.

1. Record the account balances before adjustments in the trial balance columns. Total the columns to ensure equality.
2. Enter the adjustments in the adjustments columns. Again, total the columns. Note that explanations of the adjustments are given at the bottom with corresponding numbers next to the entries in the worksheet.
3. Complete the adjusted trial balance columns by moving the amounts over from the trial balance columns. Where there are adjusting entries, they need to be combined with the trial balance amount and recorded in the adjusted trial balance columns. Total the columns to ensure continued equality.
4. Enter the amounts from the adjusted trial balance columns in the columns for the appropriate financial statement on which they appear, continuing to put debit balances in debit columns and credit balances in credit columns.
5. Determine net income by totaling the two income statement columns. The net income amount of $10,300 is then placed in the debit column as a balancing figure. Since net income increases retained earnings, it is also placed in the credit column of the retained earnings statement. Income statement columns are then totaled.
6. The retained earnings amount is determined, entered as a balance figure in the debit column of the retained earnings statement, and recorded in the credit column of the balance sheet. The retained earnings columns are totaled. Then the balance sheet columns are totaled. If they aren't in balance, an error has been made in the worksheet.

ABC Company
Worksheet
For the Year Ended December 31, 2003

(handwritten annotations: "zero", "zero", "same + adding", "Balancing figure")

Account	Trial Balance Dr	Trial Balance Cr	Adjustments Dr	Adjustments Cr	Adjusted Trial Balance Dr	Adjusted Trial Balance Cr	Income Statement Dr	Income Statement Cr	Retained Earnings Statement Dr	Retained Earnings Statement Cr	Balance Sheet Dr	Balance Sheet Cr
Cash	3,300				3,300						3,300	
Accounts receivable	4,500				4,500						4,500	
Merchandise inventory	16,200			5) 1,200	15,000						15,000	
Prepaid rent	18,000			3) 6,000	12,000						12,000	
Bond investment	12,000				12,000						12,000	
Delivery truck	6,000				6,000						6,000	
Land	15,000				15,000						15,000	
Accounts payable		25,500				25,500						25,500
Advances from customers		4,000	5) 2,000			2,000						2,000
Capital stock		27,000				27,000						27,000
Retained earnings		2,000				2,000				2,000		
Dividends	2,000				2,000				2,000			
Sales		118,000		5) 2,000		120,000		120,000				
Cost of goods sold	70,000		5) 1,200		71,200		71,200					
Salaries expense	27,000		2) 2,500		29,500		29,500					
Other expense	2,500				2,500		2,500					
	176,500	176,500										
Depreciation expense			1) 900		900		900					
Accumulated depreciation				1) 900		900						900
Salaries payable				2) 2,500		2,500						2,500
Rent expense			3) 6,000		6,000		6,000					
Interest receivable			4) 400		400						400	
Interest revenue				4) 400		400		400				
			13,000	13,000	180,300	180,300	110,100	120,400				
Net income							10,300			10,300		
							120,400	120,400			68,200	68,200
Retained earnings, Dec. 31, 2003									10,300			10,300
									12,300	12,300		

Adjustments:
1) Depreciation for year
2) December salaries
3) Rent expense for 2003
4) Interest earned on bond investment
5) Advances from customers earned, and cost of goods sold recognized

Once the financial statement worksheet is complete, adjusting entries can be journalized and posted, financial statements prepared, and closing entries journalized and posted.

If interim financial statements are prepared (such as monthly or quarterly statements), using a worksheet is best since you can prepare the statements without making formal adjusting and closing entries. These entries are done only at the end of the accounting year. When using a computer program, closing entries don't need to be prepared; most programs do it automatically when you finish a fiscal year and run the closing process. Interim statements are easily produced; again the program is able to temporarily close the books for this purpose.

Accounting Cycle

To summarize what we have learned so far, we will list in order the accounting procedures that are performed in each accounting period. This is called the accounting cycle.

1. Analyze transactions to determine the effect of the transaction on assets and equities. Then record journal entries, which provides a chronological record of the transactions of the company.
2. Post the journal entries to the ledger to accumulate the results of the transactions in the corresponding accounts.
3. Prepare an unadjusted trial balance to make sure debit and credit balances from the ledger are equal.
4. Journalize and post adjusting entries to accurately reflect the activity of the period.
5. Prepare an adjusted trial balance to again check the equality of the debit and credit balances in the ledger and to bring all the information together for the preparation of the financial statements.
6. Prepare the financial statements. The income statement shows the results of operations for the period. The statement of retained earnings shows changes during the current period and the new balance. The balance sheet shows the financial position of the company at the end of the period. The statement of cash flow shows the sources and uses of cash for the period.
7. Journalize and post closing entries to close the books for the current period.
8. Prepare an after-closing trial balance, again to verify the equality of debit and credit balances in the ledger.

Exercises ~ 12

Questions:

1. What is the accounting cycle?   List the steps.

2. What are closing entries?

3. What are temporary accounts?

4. How is a worksheet used for the end of the accounting period?

Problems:

A. Using the information from the following income statement and statement of retained earnings, prepare closing entries. You can assign your own account numbers or leave that column blank.

We Try Harder, Inc.
Statement of Retained Earnings
For the Year Ended December 31, 2005

Balance, January 1, 2005	$15,350	
Net income	8,650	
	$24,000	
Dividends	2,000	
Balance, December 31, 2005	$22,000	

We Try Harder, Inc.
Income Statement
For the Year Ended December 31, 2005

Revenues:		
Sales	$135,000	
Interest income	150	
Total revenue		$135,150
Expenses:		
Cost of goods sold	$81,000	
Salaries expense	36,000	
Insurance expense	1,500	
Other expense	5,000	
Depreciation expense	3,000	
Total expenses		126,500
Net income		$8,650
Earnings per share (9,000 shares)		$0.96

B. Given the following information and trial balance, prepare a financial statement worksheet for the year ended December 31, 2001.

Strong Company
Trial Balance
December 31, 2001

	Debit	Credit
Cash	14,500	
Accounts receivable	10,000	
Inventory	21,000	
Prepaid rent	7,000	
Bond investment	12,000	
Delivery equipment	7,500	
Accounts payable		22,500
Advances from customers		4,000
Capital stock		32,000
Retained earnings		3,500
Dividends	1,500	
Sales		96,000
Cost of goods sold	60,000	
Salaries expense	20,000	
Other expense	4,500	
	158,000	158,000

1. Depreciation on the delivery equipment for the year is $700.
2. $2,000 of the customer advances were earned with the corresponding cost of goods sold of $1,200.
3. December salaries of $2,000 were earned but not paid.
4. The portion of prepaid rent that applies to 2001 is $3,500.
5. Interest earned on the bond investment was $240.

Only the curious will learn and only the resolute overcome the obstacles to learning.
The quest quotient has always excited me more than the intelligence quotient.
~ Eugene S. Wilson

Accrual vs. Cash Accounting

Now that you understand accrual basis accounting, let's learn about another common method, cash basis accounting. In accrual basis accounting, you have learned to record revenues in the period in which they are earned and to match expenses with the revenues. It gives us an accurate picture of the company's profitability because of matching revenues and expenses to the time period in which the operating activities occurred.

Cash Basis Accounting

In cash basis accounting, on the other hand, we record transactions based on when cash is received or paid out. Revenues are recorded when cash is received. Expenses are recorded when cash is paid. Cash basis accounting doesn't give an accurate picture of the profitability of the company. This is because the cash receipts and disbursements may lead or lag the time period in which the operating activities actually occur. For this reason, cash basis accounting doesn't follow GAAP. This method can work well for small companies, individuals, and those companies for which there are little or no receivables, payables, and inventory. For most companies, however, cash basis accounting is not acceptable.

Using two companies, let's look at some examples of journal entries. Cash Co. uses cash accounting and Accrual, Inc. uses accrual accounting.

A. Sold merchandise for cash, $40,000.

Cash Co.			Accrual, Inc.		
Cash	40,000		Cash	40,000	
Sales		40,000	Sales		40,000
Cost of goods sold	25,000		Cost of goods sold	25,000	
Inventory		25,000	Inventory		25,000

B. Sold merchandise on credit in December for $35,000 Payment won't be received until January (the fiscal year ends December 31).

Cash Co.			Accrual, Inc.		
			Accounts receivable	35,000	
			Sales		35,000
			Cost of goods sold	22,000	
			Inventory		22,000

As you can see, there are no entries for Cash Co. because no money changed hands. A difficulty arises in keeping track of inventory for Cash Co. They have sold inventory but have made no entry in the books. This is part of why cash basis accounting is not appropriate for companies who carry inventory.

C. Paid two years' rent in advance of $10,000.

Cash Co.			Accrual, Inc.		
Rent expense	10,000		Prepaid rent	10,000	
Cash		10,000	Cash		10,000

As discussed previously, Accrual, Inc. will make an adjusting entry at the end of the period recognizing half of the $10,000 as expense for this period. Cash flow is the same for both companies; however, Cash Co. has $10,000 in expenses and Accrual, Inc. will only have $5,000 in expenses from this transaction.

Hopefully, you're beginning to see why accrual basis accounting is the preferred method for most businesses. To reiterate, accrual basis accounting matches revenue and expenses with the operating activities in the fiscal period. It thereby gives a more accurate reflection of the profitability of the company. Cash basis accounting does not work well in the above scenarios.

Net Cash Flow

Basically, instead of net income under cash basis accounting, we have net cash flow. Net cash flow is cash receipts minus cash expenditures. Let's look at a comparison between these two companies.

	Amount	Cash Co. Cash Receipts	Accrual, Inc. Sales Revenue
1. Cash sales this year	$40,000	$40,000	$40,000
2. Credit sales this year, cash received this year	35,000	35,000	35,000
3. Credit sales this year, cash not yet received	15,000		15,000
4. Cash received this year from last year's credit sales	8,000	8,000	_____
Total cash received		$83,000	
Total revenue			$90,000

	Amount	Cash Disbursed	Expenses
5. Cash expenses incurred this year	$7,500	$7,500	$7,500
6. Expenses incurred on credit, cash paid	6,000	6,000	6,000
7. Expenses incurred on credit, cash not paid	3,000		3,000
8. Cash paid this year for expenses incurred last year	2,500	2,500	
9. Cash paid this year for expenses to be incurred next year	1,500	1,500	
10. Expenses incurred this year, cash paid last year	3,500	_____	3,500
Total cash paid		17,500	
Total expenses			20,000
Net cash inflow		$65,500	
Net income			$70,000

Notice that net cash inflow and net income are not the same. As stated earlier, the accrual basis of accounting gives a more accurate picture of the profitability of the company. Cash basis accounting is, however, acceptable for certain companies and most individuals.

Questions:

1. What is accrual basis accounting?

matches revenues & expenses to a period when activities occurred

2. What is cash basis accounting?

only records cash receipts & disbursements

3. What are the advantages and disadvantages to accrual and cash accounting?

⊂giving an accurate picture of the businesses profitability
⊂amount of work required

Problems:

A. Prepare journal entries as needed for the following transactions for a cash basis company.

1. Paid rent in advance for two years for $8,000.
2. Purchased brochures on account for $50.
3. Received cash of $150 for services performed.
4. Purchased supplies for $75 cash.
5. Billed customer for services performed for $200.

B. Prepare a comparison chart (like the one in the chapter) for a cash basis company versus an accrual basis company for the following transactions.

1. Cash sales of $75,000.
2. Credit sales not collected of $30,000.
3. Credit sales, cash has been collected, of $25,000.
4. Cash received this year from last year's credit sales of $17,000.
5. Supplies purchased for cash for $7,500.
6. Three years' rent paid in advance of $15,000 (assume adjusting entries have been made).
7. Supplies purchased on account of $4,000.

Not everything that can be counted counts,
and not everything that counts can be counted.
~ Albert Einstein

Cash

Now that you know the basics, we're going to go into more detail about the different asset and equity accounts. This chapter will focus on the asset account, cash.

Cash

In accounting and bookkeeping, what is referred to as cash on the balance sheet is more than just the currency and coin you may have in a cash register. Cash also includes your bank balance, checks, bank drafts, money orders, etc. In short, cash is anything that a bank will accept as an immediate increase in your bank balance.

If you have multiple bank accounts, cash (currency) on hand, etc., you will have a separate ledger account to keep track of each of these. When it comes to reporting cash on the balance sheet, you will generally report one amount, the total of all of the separate cash accounts. This can be labeled anything, depending on how descriptive you wish to be, such as, "Cash in Stores and in Banks." Most of the time, it is kept simple and just called "Cash."

Periodically, cash counts should be made to maintain accuracy in the cash accounts. This helps to prevent fraud on the part of employees who handle cash. In a family business, fraud shouldn't be an issue. However, mistakes occur, so double-checking with a cash count is beneficial. If there are differences between the account balance and the physical count, the difference is recorded in the Cash Over and Short account. For example, at the end of the day, the cash register shows there should be $1,200 in the cash drawer. When the cash is counted, there is found to be $1,195. This would be recorded thus:

Cash	1,195	
Cash over & short	5	
Sales		1,200

If the cash count had been $1,207, the entry would be:

Cash	1,207	
Cash over & short		7
Sales		1,200

At the end of the accounting period, if there is a cumulative debit balance, it would be reported as a miscellaneous expense with the Cash Over & Short account credited to leave a zero balance. Conversely, a credit balance would be reported as miscellaneous revenue and the Cash Over & Short account debited to bring it to zero.

Petty Cash

Generally, cash disbursements are made by check. This ensures better control over the cash of the business. However, sometimes it is not convenient to pay by check. For example, parking fees, postage, carfares, etc. are difficult to pay by check. For these kinds of small disbursements, a petty cash fund can be set up.

To establish a petty cash fund, a check is drawn for an even amount, such as $10, $25, $50, that is large enough to last a reasonable amount of time (you don't want to be replenishing the fund every day). This check is cashed and held for making petty disbursements. The entry to record the establishment of a petty cash fund for $30 is as follows:

```
Petty cash                    30
        Cash                          30
```

When disbursements are made, receipts or other records are collected to keep track of what the money was used for. No journal entry is made until the fund is replenished.

Once the petty cash fund is nearly spent, it is time to replenish it. If $27.90 has been spent and $2.00 is left on hand, a check for $28.00 ($30 - $2) would be cashed and the following entry would be recorded.

```
Parking fees              7.50
Postage                  12.20
Office supplies           5.20
Delivery expense          3.00
Cash over & short         0.10
        Cash                    28.00
```

Notice that there is no entry to petty cash. The only time entries are made to this account is when the fund is established and when the amount of the fund is increased or decreased. The petty cash fund should be replenished at the end of a period before financial statements are prepared so that these expenditures are reported in the period in which they occurred. This follows GAAP and the matching of expenses to the period in which they occur.

Bank Accounts & Reconciliations

Separate records need to be kept for each bank account. The ledger account is a cash account although its name will likely be the name of the bank or the bank account number rather than "cash," particularly if you have more than one bank account. Cash receipts and deposits are recorded in a cash receipts journal and cash disbursements are recorded in a cash disbursements journal. At the end of each month, the totals from these two journals are recorded in the corresponding cash ledger account. The balance in the account should be the same as the bank register balance.

Since the journal totals aren't transferred until the end of the month, we need a way to know the balance in the bank during the month. One way to do this is to keep a running total on check stubs or in the checkbook register. This works fine if there isn't a large number of transactions. When there are too many transactions for this to be feasible, another method that works is the use of the bank register. Each day the total in the cash receipts journal is entered in the deposits column and the total in the disbursements journal is entered in the withdrawals column. The daily balance can then be determined. An example of a bank register follows.

Bank Register

Community Bank				National Bank			
Date 20XX	Deposits	Withdrawals	Balance		Deposits	Withdrawals	Balance
April 30			4,500				7,000
May 1	3,200	2,900	4,800		6,000	5,500	7,500
2	3,800	4,000	4,600		5,300	4,200	8,600

Once a month, the bank will send a statement. This statement shows which checks the bank has paid, the deposits made, any other withdrawals, and the balance in the account. Usually, the bank balance is not the same as the balance in the ledger. This is due to some items being recorded by the business but not yet recorded by the bank. This can include checks that have been written but haven't yet cleared through the bank. Deposits may also have been made that haven't yet been received by the bank. There also may be items recorded by the bank, but not recorded by the company. These can include service charges and charges for N.S.F. (not sufficient funds) checks. The bank will notify you immediately if there is a returned check, but the entry may not yet have been made in the books.

A bank reconciliation must be made to reconcile the difference between the bank balance and the account balance. The following elements are found on a bank reconciliation:

> The balance of the bank account on the company's books.
> Charges or credits not recorded by the company.
> Adjusted balance.
> Balance per the bank.
> Charges or credits not recorded by the bank.
> Adjusted balance.

If the two adjusted balances are the same, the bank account is considered to be reconciled. If not, an investigation needs to be made to find what is causing the difference.

These are the steps in reconciling a bank account:

> 1. Put all checks returned by the bank in numerical order.
> 2. Check off each returned check in the cash disbursements journal for this account. Some of the checks may be from a previous month.
> 3. Compare deposits recorded in the cash receipts journal with deposits on the bank statement. Check off those that appear on both. If there were deposits in transit from the previous month, they should appear on this month's bank statement.
> 4. See if there are any items on the bank statement not recorded in the company's books or items in the company's books that are not on the bank statement. These need to be shown on the bank reconciliation. A journal entry will also need to be made so that the cash account will have the correct balance for reporting on the financial statements and so that revenues and expenses are properly stated as well.
> 5. Prepare the reconciliation statement.

Here is an example of the process of preparing a bank reconciliation.

Community Bank
Statement of Account   Acct #001001

Good Company   Statement Period:
123 Front St.   From: Aug. 1, 2002
Anywhere, USA   Thru: Aug. 31, 2002

Beg. Balance	Total Withdrawals	Total Deposits	End. Balance
3,500	4,000	4,400	3,900

Date	Withdrawals	Deposits	Transaction Description
8/01		750	Customer deposit
8/05	15		Service charge
8/08		975	Customer deposit
8/12		860	Customer deposit
8/15	20		N.S. F. fee ($120.00 N.S.F.)
8/18		715	Customer deposit
8/22		675	Customer deposit
8/29		425	Customer deposit

Detail of Checks Paid:

Check #	Date Paid	Amount	Check #	Date Paid	Amount
1110	8/01	171.00	1119	8/16	555.00
1111	8/02	220.00	1120	8/15	289.50
1112	8/02	150.50	1121	8/16	64.00
1113	8/04	159.00	1122	8/16	98.00
1114	8/04	460.00	1123	8/20	799.00
1115	8/07	276.00	1124	8/23	120.00
1116	8/08	130.00	1125	8/22	77.00
1117	8/10	82.50	1126	8/25	111.00
1118	8/11	143.00	*1128	8/26	60.00

* Denotes check out of sequence.

August Cash Receipts (Journal)

Date	Explanation	Receipts	Deposits
2002			
Aug. 8	Invoice, Aug. 1	255.00	
	Invoice, July 25	350.00	
	Invoice, July 19	120.00	
	Cash sale	250.00	975.00 ✓
Aug. 12	Invoice, July 30	275.00	
	Invoice, July 31	320.00	
	Cash sale	265.00	860.00 ✓
Aug. 18	Invoice, July 21	165.00	
	Invoice, Aug. 3	210.00	
	Invoice, Aug. 4	240.00	
	Cash sale	100.00	715.00 ✓
Aug. 22	Invoice, July 29	195.00	
	Invoice, Aug. 8	230.00	
	Cash sale	250.00	675.00 ✓
Aug. 29	Invoice, Aug. 12	225.00	
	Invoice, Aug. 15	200.00	425.00 ✓
Aug. 31	Cash sale	175.00	175.00
		3,825.00	3,825.00

August Cash Disbursements (Journal)

Date	Explanation	Check #	Amount
2002			
Aug. 1	Cash purchase	1113	159.00 ✓
1	Salaries	1114	460.00 ✓
2	Invoice, July 12	1115	276.00 ✓
4	Cash purchase	1116	130.00 ✓
4	Cash purchase	1117	82.50 ✓
6	Invoice, July 15	1118	143.00 ✓
7	Rent for August	1119	555.00 ✓
9	Supplies	1120	289.50 ✓
9	Cash purchase	1121	64.00 ✓
10	Invoice, July 20	1122	98.00 ✓
13	Advertising for year	1123	799.00 ✓
16	Invoice, July 22	1124	120.00 ✓
17	Cash purchase	1125	77.00 ✓
20	Supplies	1126	111.00 ✓
21	Invoice, July 25	1127	144.00
22	Cash purchase	1128	60.00 ✓
28	Invoice, Aug. 1	1129	213.00
		4,453.00	4,453.00

Account Title Cash (Community Bank)   Account No. 101

			Ref.	Debit	Credit	Balance
2002						
July	31	Balance				4,500 Dr.
Aug	31			3,825		8,325 Dr.
	31				4,453	3,873 Dr.

Jean Claire Marinelli

Good Company
Bank Reconciliation
August 31, 2002

Balance, per books (company)		$3,873.00
Deduct:		
Service charge	$15.00	
N.S.F. fee	20.00	
N.S.F. check, G. Smith	120.00	155.00
Adjusted balance		$3,718.00
Balance, per bank		$3,900.00
Add deposit in transit		175.00
Total		$4,075.00
Deduct outstanding checks:		
1127	$144.00	
1129	213.00	357.00
Adjusted balance		$3,718.00

these no. need to agree.

Journal entry to record adjustments:

Bank fees	35	
Accounts receivable – G. Smith	120	
Cash		155

N. S .F

non suficent funds

Marinelli

Exercises – 14

Questions:
1. What is the cash over and short account used for?

to reconcile the differerets of actual cash cant & cash accounts

2. What is a petty cash fund?

cash kept available for expense that are anoying to pay a check

3. What is a bank register?

a record of total deposits/withdrawls in a accout each day to determine a daily balance

4. What is a bank reconciliation?

reconciles the balances in cash account & on a bank statement for the bank each mounth

5. What are the steps for preparing a bank reconciliation?

Problems:

A. Given the following information, prepare journal entries.

March 2 – A petty cash fund in the amount of $130 is established.

March 31 – The following is found in the fund:

Currency & coin	$17.50

Receipts for disbursements:

Postage expense	34.00
Entertainment expense	26.25
Office supplies expense	19.80
Miscellaneous expense	32.45

March 31 - The fund is replenished and increased to $150.

April 30 – The following is found in the fund:

Currency & coin	$21.00

Receipts for disbursements:

Postage expense	27.50
Travel expense	72.40
Office supplies expense	23.10
Miscellaneous expense	6.00

April 30 – The fund is replenished.

B. Given the following information,
1. Prepare a bank reconciliation (you will have to calculate the balance per books as of May 31).
2. Prepare any journal entries required.

Smith & Co. maintains a checking account with Forever Bank.
1. The balance per books as of April 30, 2003 is $2,439.10.
2. The total in the cash receipts journal for May is $6,222.00.
3. The total in the cash disbursements journal for May is $5,874.30.
4. The bank statement shows a balance of $4,243.20 on May 31, 2003.
5. Checks outstanding on May 31 are:
   No. 1341, $723.45; No. 1345, $572.10; No. 1350, $123.00;
   No. 1351, $174.50; No. 1352, $355.60; No. 1353, $61.75.
6. A deposit of $550.00 has been mailed to the bank but isn't on the bank statement.
7. The bank charged a service fee of $35.00 that the company hasn't recorded.
8. The bookkeeper recorded one of Smith & Co.'s checks, #1339, in the amount of $376.15 as $367.15; the account was Mirage Supply Co.
9. Interest of $40.00 was paid on the account balance. This has not been reccorded in Smith & Co.'s books.

Doors of opportunity don't open, they unlock; it is up to you to turn the knob.
~ Lily Taylor

Marketable Securities

When a company purchases corporate stocks or bonds or government securities for investment purposes, a decision must be made as to whether to classify them as current or long-term assets. If they are going to be held temporarily and can easily be converted into cash, they would be considered a current asset called marketable securities. Current is generally defined as short-term; usually the normal operating cycle or one year, whichever is longer. If the securities are going to be held for a long time, for example to fund future expansion, they would be classified as a noncurrent asset called long-term investments. We are going to focus on the current asset, marketable securities, in this chapter.

Marketable Equity Securities

Marketable equity securities are stocks issued by a company. They are called equity securities because you are buying equity in the company; you are an owner of the company. The original cost of an investment in securities includes the purchase price plus brokerage fees, taxes, and any other costs related to the purchase. If a company purchased 1,000 shares of Mega Company common stock at $15 per share plus purchase costs of $75, the entry to record the purchase would be as follows:

Marketable equity securities – Mega Co. common stock	15,075	
Cash		15,075

Marketable Debt Securities

The purchase of interest-bearing securities, usually bonds, work a little differently. These securities are called debt securities because they represent a debt to the issuing company – they have to pay interest on the bonds. Equity securities, i.e., common stock, do not represent a debt since the company decides if and when to pay dividends. Assume a $1,000 bond is purchased from Mega Co. on the date the bond is issued. No interest has yet accrued so the entry to record it would be as follows.

Marketable debt securities – Mega Co. bonds	1,000	
Cash		1,000

If, however, the bond is purchased between interest payments, there is an amount of interest already accrued. (Remember that on bonds interest is constantly accruing but only paid periodically.) In this case, the amount of interest accrued must be paid to the seller, then the full amount of interest will be paid to the purchaser at the next payment date. In the above example, let's assume that $50 in interest has already accrued. The journal entry to record this purchase would be:

Marketable debt securities – Mega Co. bonds	1,000	
Interest receivable	50	
Cash		1,050

Dividends and Interest Received

In recording dividends, technically they should be recognized as revenue in the period in which they are declared. However, for practical purposes, they are generally recorded as revenue when they are received. For example, if a $0.50 per share dividend is declared on the 1,000 shares of Mega Co. common stock, the following entry would be recorded when the dividend check is received:

Cash	500	
Dividend revenue		500

For interest received on bond investments, GAAP is followed by recording the interest revenue in the period in which it is earned, regardless of whether it has been paid or not. This may require an adjusting entry at the end of the period (see Chapter 11 on adjusting entries for more information). If the bond was purchased between interest payments, the interest paid to the seller is not recorded as revenue when the interest payment is received. Following are some sample journal entries to illustrate these points.

Interest was received on the bond investment, with the entire amount earned in the current period:

Cash	150	
Interest revenue		150

Interest was received on the bond investment. The purchase was made between payments with the entire amount earned in the current period so there was an amount already recorded as receivable.

Cash	150	
Interest receivable		50
Interest revenue		100

Valuation of Marketable Securities

Since the value of marketable securities changes daily, how do we report what the securities are worth on the balance sheet? The two most common methods for determining this are: lower of cost or market and cost. Either of these methods works for debt securities, but equity securities should be reported at lower of cost or market. If the market value (the amount it can be bought or sold for) is lower than the cost at the end of the period, an unrealized loss (it hasn't been sold, so the loss hasn't occurred yet) is recorded. This reduces net income for the current period. If, at the end of the next period, the market value has gone up to the original cost or higher, the loss is removed and the equity securities are shown on the balance sheet at their original cost. This adds a gain on the income statement. The maximum amount that can be shown for the combined values of all marketable securities is the total of their original costs until they are sold. The combined values of the securities are shown on the balance sheet, so we combine the individual gains and losses to determine any unrealized gains or losses to be reported.

Security	Cost	Market	Unrealized Gain (Loss)
Company A stock	$15,000	$14,000	$(1,000)
Company B stock	9,500	9,750	250
	$24,500	$23,750	$(750)

The entry to record this unrealized loss is as follows:

Unrealized loss on securities	750	
Allowance for decline in market value of marketable equity securities		750

The following year the values are:

Security	Cost	Market	Unrealized Gain (Loss)
Company A stock	$15,000	$16,500	$1,500
Company B stock	9,500	11,500	2,000
	$24,500	$28,000	$3,500

The entry would be:

Allowance for decline in market value of marketable equity securities	750	
Unrealized gain on securities		750

Remember, we can only bring the valuation of the equity securities back up to their original cost, no higher. This entry, in effect, removes the loss recorded the previous year.

This information for the first year would be shown on the financial statements in the following manner.

```
Balance Sheet
Current assets:
    Marketable equity securities                    24,500
    Allowance for decline in market value            (750)        23,750

Income Statement
Other revenues & expenses:
    Dividend revenue                                   500
    Unrealized loss on securities                     (750)
        Total other revenues & expenses               (250)
```

At the end of the second year, the balance sheet would show marketable equity securities at $24,500 with no Allowance for decline in market value. The income statement would show Unrealized gain on securities of $750 instead of the loss.

If marketable debt securities had been reduced to market value below cost and then the value had increased to cost or higher, the securities would be left at the lower amount. Once the value of debt securities are reduced on the books, they are not increased regardless of what their current market value may be. If debt securities are to be shown at cost even when the market value is lower, it is desirable to note that on the balance sheet. The idea behind this is that this is a short-term investment to be converted to cash in the near future. It's good to let the financial statement users know that less cash would be available were the debt securities to be sold immediately. This information could be shown thus:

```
Current assets:
    Marketable debt securities – at cost (market price, $35,000)        $40,000
```

Note that no accounts have been changed, this is just informational.

When the marketable securities are sold, the gain or loss is determined by the difference between the cost and the proceeds of the sale. The sale of an equity security would be recorded as follows.

```
Cash                                                10,100
    Marketable equity securities                             9,500
    Gain on sale of marketable securities                      600
```

For a bond investment being sold between interest payment dates, the interest earned would first have to be determined and recorded. Then the sale of the bonds can be recorded.

```
Interest receivable                                     75
    Interest revenue                                          75

Cash                                                 1,175
    Marketable debt securities                             1,000
    Interest receivable                                       75
    Gain on sale of marketable securities                    100
```

Exercises – 15

Questions:

1. What are marketable securities?

2. What is "current"?

3. What is the cost of marketable securities made up of?

4. What is the difference between marketable equity securities and marketable debt securities?

5. How is the value of marketable securities reported on the balance sheet?

Problem:

Given the following information for Safe & Sound Corp. for 2001,
1. Prepare journal entries to record the transactions.
2. Prepare adjusting entries including one to record the equity securities at lower of cost or market.
3. Show the presentation of the securities on the balance sheet, listing equity securities and debt securities separately.

Transactions for 2001

Jan. 5 – Bought 100 shares of A Co. stock for $75.00 per share plus brokerage
fees of $100.

Feb. 15 – Bought $5,000 face value 5% bonds of B Co. for $4,800 plus $31.25
accrued interest. Interest is payable on Jan. 1 and July 1.

Mar. 31 – Received dividends on A Co. stock of $0.75 per share.

Apr. 10 – Bought 600 shares of C Co. stock for $9.00 per share plus brokerage
fees of $75.

July 1 – Received interest on B Co. bonds.

Sept. 20 – Sold 20 shares of A Co. stock for $80.00 per share. Remember to
include brokerage fees in determining original cost.

Dec. 30 – Received dividends on C Co. stock of $0.20 per share.

Value of equities as of Dec. 31 is:

A Co. stock - $79 per share
B Co. bonds - $5,100
C Co. stock - $8.50 per share

Test 2

It is time to pause again and see how well you are retaining all of the information.

A. Prepare a financial statement worksheet for the following information for Alias Corp. for the year ended Dec. 31, 2008.

1. Balance in cash account as of Dec. 31, 2007 - $3,760.00 **A**
2. Cash receipts journal balance - $14,394.
3. Cash disbursements journal balance - $12,864.
4. Bank reconciliation shows bank fees of $25 not on books. pg 81 - 83 (bank fees) **A**
5. Accounts receivable balance - $49,000.
6. 50 shares of common stock in Equity Co. were purchased as a short-term investment at a cost of $5,000 plus brokerage fees of $150 on April 1. (ch. 15)
7. The value of the equity securities on Dec. 31 is $5,400. (ch. 15)
8. Bear Co. 6% bonds were purchased as a short-term investment on Oct. 1 for $10,000. Interest is paid on October 1 and April 1. $150
9. Beginning inventory was $8,500, purchases were $105,000, and cost of goods sold was $90,000.
10. Rent for 3 years was prepaid in 2007. The prepaid rent account was $12,000 at the beginning of 2008. **A**
11. Alias Corp. has an investment in land of $25,000.
12. Alias Corp. owns a building that cost $46,000.
13. Alias Corp. owns a delivery van. Its cost was $8,000 in 2006. It has an estimated life of 4 years and as of Dec. 31, 2007, $4,000 has been depreciated. Pg 60
14. Accounts payable balance is $26,500.
15. Alias Corp. has collected $2,000 from a customer for a special order. The order will be received in Jan. 2009.
16. Salaries owed and not recorded for December are $3,000.
17. Capital stock issued is 10,000 shares for $100,000.
18. Retained earnings balance on Dec. 31, 2007 was $27,240.
19. Dividends were paid of $250 on Dec. 31.
20. Sales for 2008 were $150,000.
21. The expense account balances were:
    Advertising - $2,400
    Office expense - $3,200
    Miscellaneous expense - $2,950
    Salaries expense - $27,000

B. Prepare a balance sheet, statement of retained earnings, income statement, and statement of cash flow for Alias Corp. from the worksheet prepared in Problem A. The following additional information is for use in preparing the statement of cash flow.

Balances as of December 31, 2007:
    Accounts receivable - $52,500
    Accounts payable - $22,000
    Salaries payable - $2,520

The rest of the beginning balances are within the information given in Problem A.

debits | credits

Much learning does not teach understanding.
~ Heraclitus

Receivables

Proper reporting of receivables and payables is important. They are reported on the balance sheet, which is used in making decisions about the liquidity of the company. If receivables or payables are understated or overstated, a wrong picture of the financial position of the company is made. This chapter will focus on receivables in more detail; the next chapter will focus on payables.

Receivables are all amounts from transactions that give a company claim to future asset inflows, usually cash. These are amounts due to the company from outside sources. Receivables arise from a variety of sources, including:

1. Amounts receivable from customers due to the sale of goods or services. They can be accounts receivable or notes receivable and can arise from sales under installment plans.
2. Amounts receivable from sales of assets that aren't merchandise.
3. Amounts receivable from money-lending activities.

The largest source of receivables for most companies is that of sales to customers. These are called trade receivables and are reported on the balance sheet as Accounts Receivable. These are the receivables we will learn about in this chapter. Assuming a sale of $1,000, the journal entry would be:

Accounts receivable	1,000	
Sales		1,000

Discounts and Returns

Sometimes sales are made at a discount. This usually happens as an incentive to customers to pay the invoice sooner rather than later. Cash discounts are stated thus: 2/10; n/30. This is read as 2% in 10 days; net 30 days. This tells the customer that they can take 2% off the invoice (pay 2% less) if they pay it within 10 days. If they don't pay it within 10 days, the full amount is due within 30 days. Cash discounts are referred to as sales discounts to the seller. We will discuss this from the buyer's point of view in the next chapter. If a company has made a $2,000 sale under the terms 1/10; n/25, the sale would be recorded as follows since we don't know whether the customer will take the discount or not.

Accounts receivable	2,000	
Sales		2,000

When the customer pays within 10 days, we record the receipt of cash in the following manner:

Cash	1,980	
Sales discounts	20	
Accounts receivable		2,000

Sales discounts are a reduction in the amount received for sales. They are therefore shown contra to sales on the income statement rather than as an expense.

Another reduction to the amount received for sales is from returns and allowances. After a customer has received some merchandise, he may not be satisfied with it, perhaps because of quality or an error in shipment. You can either have the customer return the merchandise for credit or cash, if the customer has already paid, or you can give them an allowance on the price. An allowance is a reduction in the amount the customer owes without having to return any merchandise.

For example, if a customer returns merchandise originally sold for $350 on an invoice that has not yet been paid, the journal entry to record the transaction would be as follows:

Sales returns and allowances	350	
Accounts receivable		350

The contra sales accounts would be shown on the income statement as follows:

Sales		$62,500
Deduct:		
Sales returns and allowances	$350	
Sales discounts	500	850
Net sales		$61,650

The income statement can be simplified by only showing net sales.

How do we handle a return when the invoice was paid within the discount period? The answer depends on how the customer is to be reimbursed. Let's say a customer purchased $1,000 in goods on 3/10; n/30 terms and they took advantage of the discount. They have paid $970. Now they return $200 worth of merchandise. If they are going to be paid cash, it makes sense to pay them $200 less the 3% discount, or $194, since that's all the cash they have paid out for the goods. If, on the other hand, you're going to give them credit for future purchases, the better choice would be to give them credit for the full $200 since that's the value of the goods they bought.

Credit Balance Receivables

At the end of the period, there may be individual customers who have a credit balance. The total of all accounts will still be a debit balance. On the balance sheet we do not show the individual account with the credit balance in current assets. Instead, we show the total of customer debit balances in current assets and the total of customer credit balances as a current liability. This is because a customer's credit balance is a liability to the company. The company will either pay the customer in cash or in a reduction of the amount owed on future purchases. To demonstrate, assume the following:

Total of customer accounts with debit balances	$72,000
Total of customer accounts with credit balances	(1,250)
Balance in ledger account (net receivables)	$70,750

On the balance sheet, under current assets, Accounts Receivable would be listed as $72,000. Under current liabilities would be an amount for Credit Balance of Customer Accounts of $1,250.

Bad Debts

Regardless of what procedures are in place to ensure payment by customers, it is inevitable that there will be uncollectible invoices. There are two ways to handle this: the allowance method and the direct write-off method.

The allowance method makes the assumption that since there will be some bad debts, we should reduce the amount of accounts receivable on the balance sheet to reflect the amount which will likely be collected. This has its basis in two thoughts. One is that we want to make our financial reporting as accurate as possible. It is good for the decision makers using the financial statements to know that we probably won't receive the entire accounts receivable amount. The second thought is that we are to match expenses to the period in which they occur. Bad debts are an expense for the period in which the sale originally took place since they are, in effect, reducing the amount of the sale.

There are two ways of determining what amount the entry for estimated bad debts should be. The first is associating bad debts with a percentage of the sales made on credit for that period. The second is associating bad debts with a percentage of accounts receivable, based on an aging of accounts receivable and any other pertinent data.

A company can determine an estimated percentage of sales that will be uncollectible based on its own history and current market conditions. Once this percentage is determined, it is applied to the total credit sales for the period to determine what the estimated bad debts amount is. This percentage is generally applied to net sales (sales less sales returns and allowances and sales discounts). If a company has determined that 1% of the credit sales in any given period will be uncollectible, and they have $84,000 in net sales in the current period, the estimated bad debts will be $840 ($84,000 x 0.01). The entry to record this would be:

Bad debts expense	840	
Allowance for bad debts		840

Bad debts are usually classified as an operating expense on the income statement. This journal entry is an adjusting entry made at the end of the period. Allowance for Bad Debts is a contra account to Accounts Receivable and would be shown on the balance sheet in the following manner:

Accounts receivable	$84,000	
Allowance for bad debts	840	$83,160

When a company associates bad debts with accounts receivable rather than sales, an aging of accounts receivable must be done. An accounts receivable aging shows amounts due based on age (how long it has been due), such as 1-30 days, 31-60 days, 61-90 days, etc. The older a receivable is, generally the less likely it will be collected. A percentage is determined for each age of estimated bad debts. These percentages are then applied to the aged receivables. In this method, we are adjusting the total in the Allowance for Bad Debts account. Under the percentage of sales, we don't care how much is in the contra-asset account, we just make the bad debts entry based on the percentage of sales. Under this method of connecting bad debts to accounts receivable, we will take into account what is already in the contra asset account of Allowance for Bad Debts. For example, given the following aged accounts receivable amounts and associated percentages for each age, we can determine the amount that should be in the Allowance for Bad Debts account.

Age	Amount of Accounts Receivable	Estimated % Uncollectible	Estimated Amount Uncollectible
1-30 days	$69,000	0.5%	$345
31-60 days	8,000	2.0%	160
61-90 days	4,500	6.0%	270
91 days to 6 mo.	2,000	15.0%	300
Over 6 mo.	500	35.0%	175
	$84,000		$1,250

If the amount in the allowance for bad debts account is a credit balance of $410, the entry to record estimated bad debts would be (we take the balance into consideration because we've determined the total allowance above in the schedule):

Bad debts expense	840	
Allowance for bad debts		840

When it is determined that an account can not be collected, it needs to be written off. This changes it from an allowance for bad debts to an actual reduction in Accounts Receivable. Bad debts expense is not debited; that already occurred when bad debts were estimated. Instead, the Allowance for Bad Debts is reduced. Let's say that $125 owed by Customer A is not going to be collected. The entry to record this is as follows:

Allowance for bad debts	125	
Accounts receivable		125
Amount owed by Customer A uncollectible		

If, after writing off an account as uncollectible, the customer does pay, the following entries would occur. The first is to reverse the write-off and reinstate the account. The second is to record the receipt of cash.

Accounts receivable	125	
Allowance for bad debts		125
To reverse write-off of Customer A's account		

Cash	125	
Accounts receivable		125
Receipt of amount due		

When a partial payment is received on an account that has been written off, we first have to determine if that's all we'll receive or if we'll be collecting the entire amount due. If we know that the partial payment of $45 from Customer A is all that we'll collect, the entries are:

Accounts receivable	45	
Allowance for bad debts		45
Cash	45	
Accounts receivable		45

If, however, we believe, due to information we have received, that the entire amount will be collected, the entries would be:

Accounts receivable	125	
Allowance for bad debts		125
Cash	45	
Accounts receivable		45

Rather than using an allowance for bad debts, a second method of dealing with bad debts is the direct write-off method. In this method, accounts are directly written off when they are determined to be worthless. The down side of this method is two-fold. First, the expense of the bad debt is not matched to the period in which the sale occurred. (Generally debts aren't deemed uncollectible until quite a bit of time has passed.) The second part is that there is an over-statement of the amount of receivables that are actually collectible. However, depending on the size of the company and the nature of its business, the direct write-off method may be quite acceptable.

When a bad debt is determined, the following entry is made. Remember, there is no allowance account under this method.

Bad debts expense	450	
Accounts receivable		450

If the amount is collected in the same period, the following entries occur. The first is to reinstate the account, the second is to record the cash received.

Accounts receivable	450	
Bad debts expense		450
Cash	450	
Accounts receivable		450

If the amount is recovered in a subsequent period, the following entries would be needed.

Accounts receivable	450	
Bad debt recoveries		450
Cash	450	
Accounts receivable		450

The bad debt recoveries is a revenue item that is reported on the income statement under Other Revenues.

Questions:

1. What are receivables?
all amounts from transactions that give a company claim to the future asset inflows

2. What are sales discounts ~~and how are they shown on the income statement?~~
a reduction in the amount Received for sales, usually an incentive to the customer to pay the invoice soon. they are shown as a deduction from sales on the income statement

3. What are returns and allowances and how are they shown on the income statement?
they come from customers not being satisfied purchased, returned and the customers gaining credit. returns/allowances are like sales discounts, they are a deduction from sales on the income statement

4. What are bad debts? uncollectible receivebles

5. What are the two methods of accounting for bad debts?
the allowance & direct write off

6. How are accounts receivable reported on the balance sheet when one or more customers have a credit balance? the credit balances are shown as ~~direct~~ current liability on the balance sheet. the total debit balance in receivebles is shown on the balance sheet as current assets

Problems:

A. Prepare an income statement in multiple step format from the following accounts of Goodhue Corp. for the year ended September 30, 2002. (Be aware: not all of these account balances show up on an income statement.)

Selling expense	$1,300
Cash	24,000
Sales	163,000
Allowance for bad debts (cr. balance)	11,300
Accounts receivable	37,500
Accounts payable	40,000
Sales returns and allowances	790
Office expenses	2,800
Cost of goods sold	91,000
Inventory	28,500
Bad debts expense	6,300
Sales discounts	2,100
Rent expense	4,000
Depreciation expense – Delivery vehicle	2,500
Salaries expense – Sales	32,000
Salaries expense – Administrative	15,000

B. Prepare journal entries for the following transactions of Alto Corporation (don't worry about cost of goods sold or inventory). Alto Corp. uses the direct write-off method for bad debts.

1. Sold goods to Minus Company for $600. Terms 2/10; n/30.
2. Received cash of $210 from a customer. The amount pays in full the account which was written off earlier this year as uncollectible.
3. Received a check from Plus Corp. for $727.50 within the discount period. The invoice was for $1,200 with terms of 3/10; n/30. It is Alto Corporation's policy to allow discounts on partial payment.
4. A cash refund is paid to Divisor Company for the return of one-fourth of the goods purchased. Total invoice was $1,600; terms 3/10; n/30. Divisor Company had paid within the discount period.
5. Received payment from Minus Company for invoice from #1 within the discount period.
6. It is determined that the account of Hapless Company in the amount of $550 is uncollectible.
7. A credit memo is issued to Multiple Corporation for returning one-third of the goods purchased. The invoice was for $900; terms 2/10; n/30 and was paid in the discount period. (Accounts receivable is credited even though they've already paid. It then gets classified as a liability when the financial statements are prepared.)
8. Sold goods to Divisor Company for $1,400. Terms 3/10; n/30.

C. Smith & Company has decided to use the allowance method for bad debts. The following information is taken from the books as of April 30, 2001, the end of Smith & Company's first year of business.

1. Prepare a receivables aging schedule as of April 30, 2001. Then compute the required balance in the Allowance for Uncollectibles account. Smith & Company has decided to provide for doubtful accounts as follows:

1 – 30 days	*515*	1%	*5.15*	*April 1 - 30 95, 160, 260*
31 – 60 days	*49*	4%	*1.96*	*march 1 - 31 34, 15*
61 – 90 days	*95*	12%	*11.4*	*feb 1 - 28 60, 35*
91 days – 6 months	*60*	25%	*15*	~~*Jan*~~ *nov 1 - Jan 31 60*
Over 6 months	*75*	40%	*30*	*Oct 31 + older 35 40*

2. Record the adjusting journal entry required for the above information.

Accounts Receivable Subsidiary Ledger   *63.51*   *794*

A. Brown

2001			Invoice	Receipts	Balance
Jan	3		~~90~~		90
	20	Jan 3 invoice		~~90~~	0
Feb	8		145	*35*	145
Mar	1		~~120~~		265
	17	Feb 8 invoice		110	155
Apr	11		95		250
	27	Mar 1 invoice		~~120~~	130

1-30 = 95
31 - 60 =
61 - 90 = 35
31+ = 35 ✓
91 - 6MO =
over 6 mo =

B. Cartwright

2000			Invoice	Receipts	Balance
Aug	12		235	*35*	235
	20	Aug 12 invoice		200	35
Nov	8		~~180~~		215
	15	return on Nov 8 invoice		~~80~~	135
Dec	3	Nov 8 invoice		~~100~~	35
2001					
Feb	28		260	*600*	295
Mar	15	Feb 28 invoice		200	95
Apr	1		~~195~~		290
	25			~~195~~	95

1-30 =
6+ = 35 ✓ =
31 - 60 =
61 - 90 = 60
91 - 6mo =
31+ = 60
Over 6mo = 35

C. Dwyer

2000			Invoice	Receipts	Balance
Nov	14		260	*60*	260
	30	Nov 14 invoice		200	60
2001					
Feb	1		~~175~~		235
	20	Feb 1 invoice		~~175~~	60
Mar	4		254	*34*	314
	12	return on Mar 4 invoice		120	194
	31	Mar 4 invoice		100	94
Apr	20		160	*160*	254

1 - 30 = 160
6+ = 60 ✓ 34
61 - 90 =
91 - 6mo = 60
31+ = 34 ✓
Over 6M =
60+ = 160 ✓

D. Ecklin

2000			Invoice	Receipts	Balance
July	10		~~165~~		165
Aug	2	July 10 invoice		~~165~~	0
Sept	17		290	*40*	290
Oct	10	return on Sept 17 invoice		150	140
	15	Sept 17 invoice		100	40
2001					
Jan	7		~~180~~		220
	24	Jan 7 invoice		~~180~~	40
Mar	6		~~215~~	*15*	255
	30	Mar 6 invoice		200	55
Apr	29		260	*260*	315

1 - 30 = 260
31 - 60 = 15
6+ = 40 ✓
61 - 90 =
91 - 6m =
Over 6mo = 40
31+ 15 ✓
6+ 260 ✓

We often despise what is most useful to us.
~ Aesop

Payables

Liabilities are monetary obligations of a company to outside organizations. They are either short-term, such as accounts and notes payable, or long-term, such as bonds or mortgages payable. Short-term, or current, liabilities must be paid from current assets or by the creation of other short-term liabilities within the current operating cycle or one year, whichever is longer. Most current liabilities are known as to the exact amount owed. These include cash dividends payable, rent, and interest payable. Other current liabilities aren't determined until the end of the period, such as income taxes and sales taxes payable. Some liabilities have to be estimated, such as those for liabilities under product warranties.

Accounts Payable

The most common liability is that of accounts payable. This refers to the purchase of goods, supplies, and services in the normal operations of the company. These are recurring purchases made on credit and are referred to as open accounts or open payables.

In the previous chapter, we discussed the sale of merchandise with cash discounts. Now we're going to look at this subject from the point of view of the purchaser. There are two methods for recording the purchase of merchandise when a cash discount is involved: the gross method and the net method.

Gross Method of Purchase Discounts

Under the gross method, the purchase is recorded at the invoice price. If it is paid for within the discount period, the discount would then be recorded. Purchase discounts are used to reduce inventory costs on the balance sheet. This method works well for those companies who don't routinely pay within the discount period. To illustrate this, let's assume goods are purchased for $1,500 with the terms 2/10; n/30. The purchase is recorded thus:

Inventory	1,500	
Accounts payable		1,500

When the invoice is paid within the discount period, the entry would be (this shows discounts taken):

Accounts payable	1,500	
Purchase discounts		30
Cash		1,470

If the invoice isn't paid within the discount period, we have lost the discount. The entry to record payment would be:

Accounts payable	1,500	
Cash		1,500

Keep in mind for both accounts receivable and accounts payable that there is a journal kept for each customer (accounts receivable) and vendor (accounts payable) in addition to the general ledger accounts. These individual journals added together equal the total in the ledger accounts.

Net Method of Purchase Discounts

When we use the net method, we assume that we'll pay the invoice within the discount period. Using the same information as above, we would record the purchase as follows:

Inventory	1,470	
Accounts payable		1,470

If we do, in fact, pay within the discount period, the journal entry would be:

Accounts payable	1,470	
Cash		1,470

If, however, we don't pay within the discount period, the entry would be:

Accounts payable	1,470	
Discounts lost	30	
Cash		1,500

At the end of the period, if there are any invoices on which the discount period has passed, an adjusting entry needs to be made debiting Discounts Lost and crediting Account Payable for those lost discounts.

This net method of recording purchases is beneficial for three reasons: 1) it gives management information on discounts lost so decisions can be made about payment policies; 2) it records purchases at the price at which goods can be acquired; and 3) it presents liabilities more closely to the amounts that will actually be spent. If the net method is used, it should be noted on the balance sheet that accounts payable are shown net of available discounts.

The discounts lost account can be shown in two places on the financial statements. First, it can be shown on the income statement as an administrative expense. This is based on the thought that net price is the correct measure of cost and that it's the responsibility of management to ensure that accounts are paid within the discount period. The other option for reporting discounts lost is to add the balance in this account to the inventory. The thought behind this is that cost is the entire amount paid. The choice is up to the company. Neither is wrong. However, whichever method is chosen must be applied consistently.

Questions:

1. What are liabilities?

   monetary obligations of a company to outside organizations

2. What are accounts payable?

   recurring purchase made on credit for goods, supplies & services in the normal operations of a company

3. What are purchase discounts and how are they recorded?

   they are a reduction in the amount paid for Purchases, they are recorded under gross or net paying method

4. What are discounts lost? *cash discounts on purchases that were not taken by not paying the invoice w/in the discount period*

5. What are the two ways to report discounts lost?

   admin expense on income statement

Problem: *or they can be added to inventory on balance sheet*

A. Crossover Company made the following purchases in the month of August, 2006. Determine the amount required to pay each invoice on the payment date.

Invoice Date	List Price	Credit Terms	Date of Payment
August 1	$450	2/10; n/30	August 8
7	360	1/10; n/25	August 20
16	485	2/10; n/30	August 24
21	315	3/10; n/60	September 20
28	425	3/10; n/30	September 5

B. As of December 1, 2004, the only current liability on the books of Hornblower Corporation is Accounts Payable in the amount of $9,800. Hornblower Corp. uses the net method for purchase discounts. The company's fiscal year ends on December 31. Given the following information,

    1. Prepare journal entries to record the information including any required adjusting entries.

    2. Prepare the Current Liability section of the balance sheet as of December 31, 2004.

1. Paid amount owed of $9,800 after 2% discount period expired.
2. Purchased merchandise on account for $6,200. Terms 2/10; n/30.
3. A customer paid $600 in advance for merchandise to be delivered in Feb. 2005.
4. Supplies were purchased on account for $375.
5. Merchandise was purchased on account for $7,900. Terms 3/10; n/60.
6. Cash payment was made of $6,076 on the purchase in #2. Payment was made within the discount period.
7. Dividends of $4,500 were declared.
8. Cash payment was made of $5,335 on the purchase in #5. Payment was made within the discount period. Remainder was paid in January, 2005. The discount period expired before December 31.
9. Purchased merchandise for $8,500. Terms 2/10; n/30.
10. The following amounts are owed by Hornblower Corp. on December 31, 2004.

        Salaries owed $2,500

        Rent owed for December   450

18

To live a creative life, we must lose our fear of being wrong.
~ Joseph Chilton Pearce

Inventory

In past chapters, we have recorded transactions involving purchases and sales of merchandise. Now we're going to look in more detail at how we value the merchandise inventory. This valuation is important because it affects both the balance sheet and the income statement of the company. This is seen in the following chart.

	Year 1	Year 2
Beginning inventory	$0	$2,500
Add: Merchandise purchases	18,000	24,000
Total merchandise available for sale	$18,000	$26,500
Deduct: Ending inventory (Balance Sheet)	2,500	3,000
Cost of Goods Sold (Income Statement)	$15,500	$23,500

Not only does ending inventory affect cost of goods sold in the first year, it affects it in the next as well since the ending inventory of year 1 becomes beginning inventory of year 2 and thus has an effect on cost of goods sold in year 2.

There are two methods of accounting for inventory: the perpetual inventory method and the periodic inventory method. The periodic inventory method calculates inventory from time to time, usually at the end of the period (end of the fiscal year). This method is not used that much for a number of reasons. Perhaps chief among them is the lack of timely information. Not knowing the amount of inventory on hand with any precision until the end of the year makes it difficult to make decisions related to inventory. So, we are, instead, going to focus our discussion on the perpetual inventory method.

Perpetual Inventory Method

The perpetual inventory method keeps a continuous record of the inventory on hand. All transactions involving inventory are recorded by debits and credits in the inventory account when they happen. When merchandise is purchased, it is recorded at cost with a debit to the inventory account. When merchandise is sold, its cost is credited to the inventory account. As you know from previous chapters, Cash or Accounts Payable is credited when merchandise is purchased and Cost of Goods Sold is debited when merchandise is sold. At the end of the period, the balance in the inventory account should be the value of the inventory on hand. The Cost of Goods Sold account will have the amount that will be reported on the income statement for Cost of Goods Sold for the period.

Subsidiary records are very important with the perpetual inventory method. A record needs to be kept for each type of item in inventory showing amounts purchased and sold along with the associated cost. The total of all the subsidiary inventory records then equal the total in the Inventory ledger account. With accounting software, these records are kept in the accounting system and the Inventory ledger balance is calculated from there. If you are using spreadsheets or pencil and paper, you will need to keep separate records for inventory. They could look something like this:

Item: Dinghy   Item #: D-01

	Quantity			Dollars		
Date	Purchased	Sold	Balance	Debit	Credit	Balance
20XX						
Jan. 1			3			225
7	5		8	375		600
26		2	6		150	450

Even with the perpetual inventory method, counting the physical inventory from time to time to verify its accuracy is important. If the physical inventory count and the inventory records don't match, an adjustment must be made to the records to reflect actual inventory.

Cost of Goods Available for Sale

As discussed in the previous chapter, the cost of inventory may include more than the cost of the merchandise itself. In addition to deductions for purchase discounts and returns, there can be expenses for freight, storage, insurance, duties, etc. These items are debited or credited to the inventory account as they occur. This can be seen in the following example of an Inventory ledger account.

Account Title Inventory   Account No.

		Ref.	Debit	Credit	Balance
20XX					
	Beginning inventory				12,000 Dr.
	Purchase		43,000		55,000 Dr.
	Freight in		1,750		56,750 Dr.
	Purchase returns & allowances			2,000	54,750 Dr.
	Purchase discounts			430	54,320 Dr.
	Sales			39,000	15,320 Dr.

The cost of goods available for sale is the amount of inventory at the beginning of the period plus any purchases. This is the amount of inventory that can be sold during the period. At the end of the period, some has been sold and some is still on hand. There are several ways of allocating the cost of goods available for sale between the cost of goods sold and the cost of goods still on hand. This allocation occurs throughout the period as merchandise is bought and sold. Each business must determine which method of inventory valuation works best for their circumstances. The four most common methods of inventory valuation are: specific identification; weighted-average; first-in, first-out; and last-in, first-out. For the following discussions of the different inventory valuation methods, assume the following:

	Units	Unit Cost
Beginning inventory	3	$20
First purchase	1	24
First sale	1	
Second purchase	2	20
Third purchase	1	22
Second sale	2	
Third sale	2	
Fourth purchase	1	24

Specific Identification Method

Specific identification works best for companies with unique items for which the cost can be associated with individual items. Using the above information, if the first sale was one of the items in inventory at the beginning of the period, the cost of goods sold would be $20.

Weighted-Average Method

The weighted-average method is the most complicated method since a new average is calculated every time there is a sale. This method works well for those companies whose goods are hard to differentiate, such as a hardware store. For example, when the first sale is made, the following calculations would occur:

Cost of goods available for sale:
3 units @ $20 (beg. inventory)	$60.00	
1 unit @ $24	24.00	$84.00
Total units available for sale		4
Average unit cost ($84.00 ÷ 4)		$21.00

The unit sold is recorded at a cost of $21.00 with the remaining units in inventory at a total cost of $63.00 (84.00 – 21.00). When the second sale occurs, its cost is calculated thus:

Cost of goods available for sale:

3 units @ $21	$63.00	
2 units @ $20 (2ⁿᵈ purchase)	40.00	
1 unit @ $22 (3ʳᵈ purchase)	22.00	$125.00
Total units available for sale		6
Average unit cost ($125.00 ÷ 6)		$20.83 (rounded)

The units sold are recorded at a total cost of $41.66 with the remaining inventory at a cost of $83.34 (125 – 41.66).

First-In, First-Out Method

The first-in, first-out (FIFO) method assigns cost to inventory using the oldest cost first. This leaves the value of the inventory at the most recent purchase price(s). This works well for those companies that sell the oldest inventory first, such as perishable goods. It is also good merchandising practice to sell the oldest goods first. The first unit sold would have a cost of $20 since it would be considered to have come out of beginning inventory. That leaves us with the following inventory at the time of the second sale:

2 units @ $20 (beg. inventory)	$40.00
1 unit @ $24 (1ˢᵗ purchase)	24.00
2 units @ $20 (2ⁿᵈ purchase)	40.00
1 unit @ $22 (3ʳᵈ purchase)	22.00

The second sale would have a cost of $40 (the remaining 2 items in beginning inventory). The third sale would have a cost of $44 (the 1st unit purchased for $24 and one of the units from the second purchase for $20).

Last-In, First-Out Method

The last-in, first-out (LIFO) method assigns cost to inventory in reverse of FIFO. The most recent purchase determines the amount of cost of goods sold. This leaves the value of inventory at the older purchase prices. In our example, the first unit sold would have a cost of $24, the amount at which a unit had just been purchased. The second sale would have recorded cost of goods sold at $42, one unit from the 3rd purchase at $22 and one unit from the 2nd purchase at $20.

In addition to the valuation of inventory varying from method to method, the company's gross margin and net income amounts also would be different. Once an inventory valuation method is chosen, it must be applied consistently from period to period.

There are many factors that go into deciding which inventory method to use. In the 1970's the LIFO method was popular because, due to rising prices, it reduced the company's net income, thereby reducing income taxes and increasing the cash available for expansion. To illustrate the difference in gross margin and ending inventory between FIFO and LIFO, assume the company has one unit in inventory at a value of $100. Its sales price is $140. Before making a sale another unit is purchased for $115. The company decides it must raise its selling price to $160. It then sells one unit for $160.

	FIFO	LIFO
Sale	$160	$160
Cost of inventory sold	100	115
Gross margin	$60	$45
Ending inventory	$115	$100

Exercises ~ 18

Questions:

1. Why is how we value inventory important?

2. What is the perpetual inventory method?

3. What is the cost of goods available for sale?

4. What are the four most common methods of inventory valuation?

Problem:

A. Corporal Corporation had the following transactions in May, 2003. Calculate the following under both the FIFO and LIFO methods.
1. Inventory reported on the balance sheet as of May 31, 2002.
2. Cost of goods sold for the month.

May 1 Balance, 200 units @ $15 each.
    3 Purchased 100 units @ $17 each.
    8 Sold 125 units @ $30 each.
  12 Purchased 150 units @ $18 each.
  20 Sold 75 units @ $35 each.
  28 Sold 150 units @ $35 each.

B. Jones Company had a beginning inventory of 150 units, costing $5 per unit on October 1, 2002. The following purchases and sales occurred during the month. Calculate the ending inventory by each of the following inventory valuation methods.
1. Weighted average pg 102
2. First-in, first-out
3. Last-in, first-out

Date		Quantity	Unit Cost
Oct. 2	Purchase	100	$5
7	Sale	125	
11	Purchase	150	7
18	Purchase	100	8
23	Sale	200	
26	Purchase	100	8

C. Given the following information for Hi-Tech Corporation for 2003, calculate the following under both FIFO and LIFO.
1. Cost of goods sold o
2. Gross margin
3. Net income

Marinelli

Sales	$250,000
Purchases	148,000
Purchase returns & allowances	7,500
Purchase discounts	6,000
Transportation in	1,250
Beginning inventory	24,000
Ending inventory, FIFO	26,000
Ending inventory, LIFO	23,500
Other expenses	52,000

16 C 1 & 2
17 B 2

19

Kites rise highest against the wind -- not with it.
~ Sir Winston Churchill

Long-lived Assets

Long-lived assets are those assets which are purchased for use in the business, rather than for resale, and are generally expected to be used for many years. The most commonly recognized category of long-lived assets is property, plant, and equipment. This includes land, buildings, machinery, vehicles, etc.

Valuation of Property, Plant, and Equipment

The cost of the asset at its acquisition is its value to the company; therefore that is what is recorded in the books of the company. The cost includes all expenditures related to the purchase of the asset, to putting it in place, and to getting it in the condition it needs to be in, in order to use it. For example, a machine was invoiced at $4,000 with a 3% discount for paying within 10 days (which the company does). The company also pays $200 in freight charges and $350 for installation. We would calculate the cost and record the transaction as follows:

Invoice price	$4,000	
Less 3% discount	120	
Net invoice price	$3,880	
Add: freight	200	
installation	350	
	$4,430	
Equipment	4,430	
Cash		4,430

If land and a building are purchased together, separate records must be kept since land doesn't get depreciated, while a building does. The cost must be assigned between the two. This can be done based on an appraisal at the time of purchase. If, for example, you purchase some land with a warehouse on it for $125,000 and the appraisal shows the value of the land to be $30,000 and the building $120,000, the costs would be determined by calculating the percent of the value attributable to the land and the building. These percentages can then be applied to the total cost to arrive at the separate costs for the land and the building.

	Appraisal	%	Cost
Land	30,000	20%	25,000
Building	120,000	80%	100,000
	150,000		125,000

This same procedure can be applied any time more than one asset is purchased for a single price.

Land

When land is purchased, all costs associated with the purchase and with making it suitable for use are charged to the land account. This includes brokerage fees, recording title, surveying, clearing, and landscaping. If there is a building on the land that is unsuitable, the cost of the building is charged to the land account, as well as the cost of removal less any salvage. If there are any accrued interest or taxes paid at the time of purchase, these are also considered part of the cost of the land. Again, if there are improvements (i.e., buildings) on the land that are going to be used by the company, the accrued interest and taxes would be divided between the land and the improvements.

Buildings

Any remodeling, renovating, or other improvements to a building should be added to the cost of the building. If a building is being built for the company, the costs associated with the project, such as contractor's fees, building permits, architects' fees, insurance, and interest on the construction loan, are charged to the building account.

Depreciation

We do not expect the things that man has made to last forever. They wear out or become obsolete. You understand the concept of things wearing out. I'll give you a couple of examples to illustrate the concept of obsolescence. Let's say you have a machine that makes 50 units a day but now you want to make 500 units a day. Instead of buying ten more machines, you buy a machine that can make 500 units a day. The 50 units a day machine is now obsolete. A second example would be that the item this machine makes is no longer marketable (no one will buy this item any more). Since the machine can only make this item, it is obsolete.

This brings us to depreciation. Depreciation spreads the cost of an asset over the years of its useful life in a systematic manner, allowing the company to recover part of the cost of the asset in each year it is used. The total amount to be depreciated over the life of an asset varies depending on whether an amount for salvage at the end of the asset's useful life is taken into consideration or not. If the company expects to be able to recover some of the cost of the asset when it is disposed of, total depreciation is the cost minus the salvage amount. If not, the total cost is depreciated. Either way is acceptable. Depreciation only applies to those things that wear out, get used up, or become obsolete. Therefore, land, which does none of these things, is never depreciated.

Straight-Line Method of Depreciation

There are many depreciation methods. We are just going to focus on one – the straight-line method. We have already discussed this method of depreciation in a previous chapter so we will just review it now. Depreciation is determined by dividing the cost of an asset by the number of years it is estimated to be useful. For example, suppose you have a machine which cost $8,000, has a useful life of 10 years, and a salvage value of $800. If you are going to take salvage value into account, then the annual amount of depreciation would be $720 ($8,000 - $800 = $7,200 ÷ 10 = $720). If you want to depreciate the entire cost of the machine, the depreciation per year would be $800 ($8,000 ÷ 10 = $800). The annual depreciation rate in both of these examples is 10% (1.00 ÷ 10).

Depreciation is recorded as a debit to depreciation expense and a credit to the contra-asset account, accumulated depreciation. From the first example above, the annual journal entry would be:

Depreciation expense	720	
Accumulated depreciation		720

The asset account doesn't change unless additional costs are added (such as from improvements) or the asset is disposed of. At the end of the third year in the first example above, the balance sheet would show the following:

Long-lived assets:		
Equipment	$8,000	
Less accumulated depreciation	2,160	$5,840

The difference between the asset and the contra-asset accounts is the carrying amount, often referred to as the book amount or book value. Once an asset is fully depreciated, i.e., the amounts in the asset and accumulated depreciation accounts are equal (or there is a difference of the amount of salvage value), no further depreciation is recorded and the accounts stay as they are until the asset is disposed of.

Disposal of Depreciable Assets

When a depreciable asset is disposed of, the first thing to do is to make sure that the amount of depreciation is correct. If an asset is disposed of on Jan. 1, 2001 and depreciation was recorded on Dec. 31, 2000 (the end of the fiscal year), then no further entry for depreciation need be recorded. If, on the other hand, an asset is sold on March 31, 2001 and depreciation hasn't been recorded since Dec. 31, 2000, an adjusting entry needs to be made. Let's say the asset has a cost of $15,000 and is being depreciated over 10 years with no salvage value. It was originally purchased on Jan. 1, 1995. Before recording its sale on March 31, 2001, we must record depreciation for three months (3/12 of a year). The amount would be $375 ($15,000 ÷ 10 x 3/12) with the following journal entry made:

Depreciation expense	375	
Accumulated depreciation		375

If the asset is sold for book value, the entry would be:

Cash	5,625	
Accumulated depreciation	9,375	
Equipment		15,000

If the asset is sold for less than book value, there is a loss on the sale.

Cash	4,500	
Loss on disposal of equipment	1,125	
Accumulated depreciation	9,375	
Equipment		15,000

5625

If the asset is sold for more than book value, there is a gain on the sale.

Cash	6,000	
Accumulated depreciation	9,375	
Equipment		15,000
Gain on disposal of equipment		375

Intangible Assets

Some assets owned by a company have no physical substance and yet they still have value. These include patents, franchises, leaseholds, and goodwill. These are referred to as intangible assets. Like tangible assets (machinery, buildings, etc.), intangible assets have a limited life. Therefore, the cost of these assets is expensed over time. This expensing of intangible assets is called amortization.

The cost of an intangible asset is determined in much the same way as tangible assets. Sometimes they are purchased from outside sources and sometimes they are developed within the company. The amortization amount is calculated in the same way as depreciation. The length of its useful life is dependent upon the length of contract (as with franchises and leaseholds) or the length of issuance (as in patents). Goodwill is a much more complicated and ambiguous asset, which is beyond the scope of this book.

```
 5000
+ 250
+ 650
 1400  - 600 = 800 ÷ 8 = 100
5900 - 600 = 5300 ÷ 8 = 662.50
```

Exercises – 19

Questions:

1. What are long-lived assets?

2. How do we value long-lived assets? *is the cost to purchase the asset to put it in place to get it in conditing required for use.*

3. If we purchase multiple assets for a single amount, how do we determine the value of each? *we asign a portion of the purchase price to each asset based on the percentage detarmined by an aprisal.*

4. What is depreciation?

5. What is the straight-line method of depreciation?

6. What is an intangible asset?

Problem:

A. Bamboo Corporation purchased a widget machine on Jan. 1, 2002 for $5,000. They paid $250 on freight charges and $650 to have it installed. They expect it to last for 8 years with a salvage value of $600. Calculate the annual amount of depreciation taking salvage value into account.

B. Gloomis Company acquired some land with a building on Aug. 1, 2003 for $175,000. The appraised value of the land was $40,000 and the building was $160,000. Additional landscaping was performed for $3,000. Improvements to the building to make it suitable were made for $10,000. It is determined that the building has a useful life of 30 years.

1. Calculate the cost of the land and the building to be recorded in the company's books. *388000*
2. Determine the amount of depreciation to be recorded for 2003 and 2004. *25,866.66 10000*
3. On Dec. 1, 2020, the land and building are sold for $215,000. *2003 - 2020 = 17 yrs (dep = 219,866.66)*
   a. Record the journal entry for depreciation for 2020. *4583.33*   *+215 000.00*
   b. Determine the profit or loss on the sale and record the journal entry for the sale. *86666.66 434,866.66*

2003 - 2083.33

101,333.34$

I never let schooling interfere with my education.
~ Mark Twain

Other Forms of Business

We have been using corporations for our examples in this book. Now we are going to look at the differences between corporations and other forms of organizing a business.

Corporation

First, let's define a corporation. A corporation is a legal entity (the same as a person in the legal system). It can be owned by one or more individuals, or even other corporations. Each owner holds shares of stock in the corporation. They can vote on issues involved in operating the company, but they do not have direct control as do sole proprietors or partners. A corporation is run by officers who report to a board of directors who are, in turn, elected by the stockholders. The corporation itself pays taxes on any profits. There are various ways of establishing a corporation, such as C, S, or not-for-profit. Each one has benefits and drawbacks.

Sole Proprietorship

A sole proprietorship is a business entity in which an individual is the owner and operator of the business. All of the risks and all of the profits, or losses, belong to this individual. Business is conducted under the owner's name or under an assumed name, which must be registered with the state in which the business operates. The sole proprietor is taxed as if the profits or losses were his income, whether or not he pays himself this entire amount. This income is reported on his personal income tax return.

The only place that we see a difference between a corporation and a sole proprietorship from an accounting perspective is in the equity accounts. Instead of capital stock, retained earnings, and dividends, a sole proprietorship has a capital account and a drawing account.

The capital account is credited for all amounts that the owner puts into the business. It is also credited with net income or debited with net loss at the end of each period. The drawing account is used for the withdrawals of the owner. This includes cash and business assets (such as merchandise for personal use). Withdrawals recorded in the drawing account would also include amounts paid by the business for the owner's personal use (such as making the mortgage payment on the owner's home) and any collections of accounts for the business that are deposited in the owner's personal account. At the end of the period, the drawing account is closed to the capital account.

Following are examples of the capital and drawing ledger accounts as well as the financial statements and closing entries for a sole proprietorship.

Account Title   Harold Crinkle, Capital   Account No.

2003			Ref.	Debit	Credit	Balance
Jan	1	Investment			8,000	8,000 Cr.
Apr	15	Additional investment			3,000	11,000 Cr.

Account Title   Harold Crinkle, Drawing   Account No.

2003			Ref.	Debit	Credit	Balance
May	1			600		600 Dr.
July	7			1,350		1,950 Dr.
Oct	22			1,900		3,850 Dr.
Dec	3			1,650		5,500 Dr.

Harold Crinkle
Balance Sheet
December 31, 2003

Assets		Equities		
Current assets:		Current liabilities:		
Cash	$4,000	Accounts payable	$7,500	
Accounts receivable	11,500	Notes payable	12,000	$19,500
Inventory	25,000			
Total assets	$40,500	Owner's equity:		
		Harold Crinkle, capital		21,000
		Total equities		$40,500

Harold Crinkle
Statement of Owner's Equity
For the Year Ended December 31, 2003

Owner's equity, January 1, 2003		$8,000
Add:		
Additional investment	$3,000	
Net income for year	15,500	18,500
Total		$26,500
Deduct withdrawals		5,500
Owner's equity, December 31, 2003		$21,000

Harold Crinkle
Income Statement
For the Year Ended December 31, 2003

Sales		$72,000
Sales returns & allowances		1,500
Net sales		$70,500
Cost of goods sold	$40,000	
Operating expenses	15,000	55,000
Net income		$15,500

Closing Journal entries:

Sales	72,000	
Sales returns & allowances		1,500
Cost of goods sold		40,000
Operating expenses		15,000
Harold Crinkle, capital		15,500
To close revenue and expense accounts and transfer net income to capital account		
Harold Crinkle, capital	5,500	
Harold Crinkle, drawing		5,500
To close the drawing account		

Partnership

A partnership is owned by two or more people or entities. Each owner owns a percentage of the business, not necessarily an equal division. They may or may not be involved in the day-to-day operations of the business. The partners are individually responsible for the acts of the business much as a sole proprietor is for his. Each partner has a capital and a drawing account to record the assets contributed to or withdrawn from the business. The profits are reported, for income tax purposes, to each partner according to the percentage of ownership. Again, like the sole proprietorship, this is the entire amount of profit, or loss, not the amount taken out of the business as compensation. These are then reported on the partner's personal income tax return. As in the corporation, there are various ways in which to form a partnership, with differing benefits.

The books of the partnership are kept in the same way as a sole proprietorship, just with multiple capital and drawing accounts. To record the original investment, the journal entry would look something like this:

```
Cash                                    36,000
     W. Smith, capital                           20,000
     K. Jones, capital                           16,000
     To record original investment
```

If the two partners previously had sole proprietorships and are combining their businesses, the entry to record the initial investment would be:

```
Cash                                    18,000
Accounts receivable                     12,000
Inventory                                7,500
     Accounts payable                            17,500
     W. Smith, capital                           20,000
     To record initial investment of partner


Cash                                    12,000
Delivery truck                           8,000
Inventory                                5,000
     Accumulated depreciation, truck              2,000
     Accounts payable                             7,000
     K. Jones, capital                           16,000
     To record initial investment of partner
```

If the partners do not specify how to allocate the net income or loss, it is assumed to be split equally. The income statement looks the same as that of any other business, except that the allocation of net income may be shown.

Smith & Jones
Income Statement
For the Year Ended December 31, 2003

Sales		$125,000
Sales returns & allowances		2,000
Net sales		$123,000
Cost of goods sold	$80,000	
Operating expenses	33,000	113,000
Net income		$10,000
Allocation of net income:		
W. Smith – 60%	$6,000	
K. Jones – 40%	4,000	$10,000

A partnership has a statement of partners' capitals in place of the corporation's statement of retained earnings. Because each partner's capital is shown, it is necessary to refer to the capital and drawing ledger accounts for all partners.

Smith & Jones
Statement of Partners' Capitals
For the Year Ended December 31, 2003

	W. Smith	K. Jones	Total
Investment, January 1, 2003	$20,000	$16,000	$36,000
Add:			
Additional investment	3,000	3,000	6,000
Net income	6,000	4,000	10,000
Totals	$29,000	$23,000	$52,000
Deduct withdrawals	2,500	2,000	4,500
Balance, December 31, 2003	$26,500	$21,000	$47,500

The balance sheet shows each partner's capital amount in the equity section.

Smith & Jones
Balance Sheet
December 31, 2005

Assets			Equities		
Current assets:			Current liabilities:		
Cash	$17,000		Accounts payable		$11,000
Accounts receivable	28,000		Owner's equity:		
Inventory	8,500	$53,500	W. Smith, capital	$26,500	
Long-term assets:			K. Jones, capital	21,000	47,500
Delivery truck	$8,000		Total equities		$58,500
Accumulated depreciation	3,000	5,000			
Total assets		$58,500			

Closing the books follows the same pattern as we have seen before.

Sales	125,000	
Sales returns & allowances		2,000
Cost of goods sold		80,000
Operating expenses		33,000
W. Smith, capital		6,000
K. Jones, capital		4,000
To close the revenue and expense accounts and transfer net income to partners' capital accounts		
W. Smith, capital	2,500	
W. Smith, drawing		2,500
To close the drawing account		
K. Jones, capital	2,000	
K. Jones, drawing		2,000
To close the drawing account		

Limited Liability Company (LLC)

A limited liability company is very similar to a partnership. It is comprised of partners, or members (whether they be individuals, corporations, etc.), who have joined together to do business. The profits, or losses, are allocated among the partners for income tax purposes in the same manner as a partnership. The big difference between the two is that the liability for the actions of the business is limited in an LLC (similar to the owners of a corporation having limited liability for the actions of a corporation); whereas in a partnership, the partners bear full responsibility for the actions of the business. If the LLC acts more like a corporation, however, it can be classified as one for tax purposes. This would be determined at the time the LLC is formed.

The books of an LLC are set up in the same way as a partnership with a capital and drawing account for each member. The examples previously shown for a partnership would also apply to an LLC.

Questions:

1. What is a sole proprietorship?

2. What equity accounts are used in a sole proprietorship?
   capital account + drawing account

3. What is a partnership?

4. What equity accounts are used in a partnership?

5. What is a limited liability company?
   is a partnership w/ limited liability to the partner.

6. How does an LLC differ from a partnership?

Problem:

A. Given the following account information, prepare a balance sheet, statement of owner's equity, income statement, and ~~cash flow~~ statement for the sole proprietorship of Ralph Smart for the year 2001.

pg. 109 - 110

	12/31/2000	12/31/2001
Sales		$95,000
Sales discounts		750
Cost of goods sold		55,000
Rent expense		6,000
Office expense		4,000
Miscellaneous expense		1,500
Depreciation expense		1,000
Owner's equity	$1,000	
R. Smart, drawing		6,000
Cash	+ 11,000	17,000 → *18,000*
Accounts receivable	+10,000	12,000
Inventory	- 12,000	16,000
Delivery truck	- 7,000	7,000
Accumulated depreciation	- 2,000	3,000
Accounts payable	-27,000	21,000
Note payable (short-term)	- 10,000	7,250

B. Given the following account information, prepare a balance sheet, statement of members' capitals, income statement, and ~~cash flow statement~~ for Yankee Doodle, LLC for 2003. The members share profits equally.

pg. 110 - 112

	12/31/2002	12/31/2003
Sales		$174,000
Sales returns & allowances		4,000
Cost of goods sold		110,000
Salaries expense		17,000
Salaries payable		2,500
Office expense		5,000
Miscellaneous expense		3,000
Depreciation expense		2,000
G. Washington, capital 1/1/03	$18,000	
G. Washington, drawing		2,500
P. Revere, capital 1/1/03	17,500	
P. Revere, drawing		3,000
T. Jefferson, capital 1/1/03	17,500	
T. Jefferson, drawing		2,000
Cash	54,500	32,000
Accounts receivable	28,000	25,000
Inventory	15,500	14,500
Land	5,500	5,500
Building	0	60,000
Accumulated depreciation	0	2,000
Accounts payable	48,000	50,000
Advances from customers	0	4,000

Marinelli

Learning is not attained by chance, it must be sought for with ardor
and attended to with diligence.
~ Abigail Adams

Payroll

Once a company has employees, it has a payroll. It is important that you keep accurate payroll records. These records are used to determine the amount to pay each employee and how much to pay the various taxing authorities. Payroll accounting can quickly become very complicated. This chapter is going to deal with the recording of the payroll and the taxes that are associated with it. The taxing authorities involved with collecting employment taxes are happy to give you detailed information as to how much to collect, when to send it to them and what forms to fill out to go with the money.

Before getting any further into this chapter, let's define some acronyms used.

flashcards

FICA – OASDI = Federal Insurance Contribution Act for old-age, survivors, and disability insurance (Social Security)
FICA – HI = Federal Insurance Contribution Act for hospital insurance (Medicare)
FIT = Federal Income Tax
SIT = State Income Tax
FUTA = Federal Unemployment Tax Act
SUTA = State Unemployment Tax Act

Payroll Register

The payroll register is the initial place to record all of the earning information for each employee in each payroll period. This record may be kept by hand (preprinted business forms are available) or on the computer (accounting software packages generally include payroll). The following information would be included: name of employee, employee number, marital status, number of hours worked, regular and overtime earnings, deductions for FICA, FIT, SIT, insurance premiums (and other deductions the employee agrees to such as 401-K contributions), net amount paid, and check number. A sample of a payroll register is on the next page.

In addition to the payroll register, an earnings record needs to be maintained for each employee. These records are used in completing the payroll register each pay period as well as accumulating the cumulative earnings of each employee. This additional information of cumulative earnings is used in reporting wage information on form W-2 at the end of the year to each employee for filing their tax returns. An example of an earnings record is also on the next page.

The journal entries to record payroll are made from the information in the payroll register. Before recording the journal entries, however, the payroll register must be proven. This is done by verifying that the total earnings equal the net pay plus the withholdings. Using the information from the sample payroll register, the proof would be prepared as follows:

Regular earnings	$3,000	
Overtime earnings	250	
Total earnings /gross earnings		$3,250
FICA tax withheld – OASDI	$200	
FICA tax withheld – HI	50	
FIT withheld	225	
SIT withheld	125	
Total deductions		$600
Total net pay		2,650
Total earnings		$3,250

FOR WEEK ENDING FEBRUARY 25, 20XX

	EMP. NO.	NAME	MARITAL STATUS	WITHHOLDING ALLOWANCE	S	M	T	W	T	F	S	REG. HOURS	RATE PER HOUR	AMOUNT	OT HOURS	RATE PER HOUR	AMOUNT	TOTAL EARNINGS	OASDI	HI	FEDERAL INCOME TAX	STATE INCOME TAX	INSURANCE	CHECK NUMBER	NET AMOUNT	OASDI	HI	FUTA & SUTA
1	12	Pickrel, Margret	M	7		8.0	8.0	8.0	8.0	8.0	6.0	40.00	19.00	760.00	6.00	28.50	171.00	931.00	26.53	4.42	33.00	11.00	0.00	1447	856.05	931.00	931.00	931.00
2	14	Spade, Sam	M	3	8.0	8.0	6.0	8.0	8.0	8.5		38.50	18.00	693.00				693.00	20.19	3.37	24.50	8.17	0.00	1448	636.78	693.00	693.00	693.00
3	25	Howard, Cal	S	1	1.0	8.0	0.0	9.5	0.0	0.0		18.50	23.00	425.50				425.50	12.57	2.09	16.77	5.59	0.00	1449	388.48	425.50	425.50	425.50
4	29	Shovel, Roy	M	3	3.0	0.0	8.0	8.0	8.0	0.0		27.00	18.00	486.00				486.00	13.98	2.33	17.90	5.97	0.00	1450	445.82	486.00	486.00	486.00
5	32	Green, Petunia	S	0	1.0	4.0	0.0	8.0	8.0	8.0		21.00	15.00	315.00				315.00	9.45	1.58	13.60	4.53	0.00	1451	285.84	315.00	315.00	315.00
		TOTALS												3000.00			250.00	3250.00	200.00	50.00	225.00	125.00	0.00		2650.00	3250.00	3250.00	3250.00

EMPLOYEE'S EARNINGS RECORD

WEEK	WEEK	DAYS	HRS	HRS	HRS	RATE	AMOUNT	HRS	RATE	AMOUNT	TOTAL PERIOD GROSS	OASDI	HI	FEDERAL INCOME TAX	STATE INCOME TAX	INSURANCE	TOTAL DEDUCTIONS	CHK. #	AMOUNT	TOTAL EARNINGS TO DATE
1	1/3/2004	4	32	32	32	25.00	800.00	0.0	37.50	0.00	800.00	40.00	24.00	160.00	24.00	36.00	284.00	10129	516.00	110,563.27
2	1/10/2004	5	42	42	40	25.00	1,000.00	2.0	37.50	75.00	1,075.00	53.75	32.25	215.00	32.25	36.00	369.25	10543	705.75	111,269.02
3	1/17/2004	7	60	60	40	25.00	1,000.00	20.0	37.50	750.00	1,750.00	87.50	52.50	350.00	52.50	36.00	578.50	10958	1,171.50	112,440.52
4	1/24/2004	4	32	32	32	25.00	800.00	0.0	37.50	0.00	800.00	40.00	24.00	160.00	24.00	36.00	284.00	11111	516.00	112,956.52
13 QUARTER TOTAL																				
SEMIANNUAL TOTAL																				

EMPLOYEE INFORMATION

| SEX: F | DEPT.: Eng. | OCCUPATION: DRAFTER | WORKS IN STATE: AK | SOC. SEC.: XXXX-XXX-XXXX | LAST: Dunkmeister | FIRST: Glory | M.I. B. | MARRIED: Y | W/H ALLOWANCE: 6 |

In the journal entry for payroll, the earnings are recorded as wages expense and the taxes withheld are recorded in the appropriate liability (payable) accounts. The above payroll activity would be recorded as follows:

```
Wages expense                              3,250
     FICA taxes payable – OASDI                      200
     FICA taxes payable – HI                          50
     FIT payable                                     225
     SIT payable                                     125
     Cash                                          2,650
  To record wages expense and withholdings
```

Employer Taxes

The taxes withheld from employees' wages are not taxes on the business. They are just being collected from the employee and passed on to the appropriate taxing authority. There are, however, employment taxes that a business pays that aren't withheld from the employees' wages. These are separate from the wages expense of the business. These taxes include the employer's share of FICA – OASDI and HI as well as FUTA and SUTA. Following is the journal entry to record these taxes for the period.

```
Payroll taxes                              355
     FICA taxes payable – OASDI                      200
     FICA taxes payable – HI                          50
     FUTA taxes payable                               25
     SUTA taxes payable                               80
  To record payroll taxes
```

When these taxes are paid, the following journal entry is made.
Note: There would actually be multiple entries - one each for paying the taxes to the separate taxing authorities. For simplicity in illustration, we have combined them into one.

```
FICA taxes payable – OASDI                 400
FICA taxes payable – HI                    100
FUTA taxes payable                          25
SUTA taxes payable                          80
FIT payable                                225
SIT payable                                125
     Cash                                          955
  Payment of payroll taxes
```

End-of-Period Adjustments

At the end of the period, any wages that have been earned but not yet paid must be recorded as an expense and a liability. Only the wages are recognized; no entry needs to be made for any withholding accounts until the wages are actually paid. For example, the company pays wages every other Friday and the fiscal year ends on the Wednesday before payday. The wages for the last eight working days must be recognized as expense. If the employees earn $200 per day, the entry would be as follows:

```
Wages expense                              1,600
     Wages payable                                 1,600
  To record wages incurred but not paid at end of fiscal period
```

Note that the entire amount of earnings is accrued as an expense and a liability. This entry would be reversed at the beginning of the new fiscal period and the full two weeks' wages would be recorded normally on Friday.

Exercises – 21

Questions:

1. What is a payroll register?

   the initial place to record all of the earning info for each employee in each payroll period

2. What are some of the withholdings from employees' wages?

   Liability (account) payable — FICA, FIT + SIT + insurance premiums, + 401-k contrib, etc

3. What are some taxes paid by employers?

   FICA + OASDI + HI. + Futa + Suta

Problems:

A. Given the following information, determine the net pay for the current period for McCorkle's Cork Company.

Regular earnings	$2,500
Overtime earnings	350
FICA taxes – OASDI	175
FICA taxes – HI	40
FIT	190

B. Using the information in Problem A (and your answer), prepare a proof of the payroll register. *pg. 115*

C. Given the following information for Simply Super Stamp Company, prepare the necessary journal entries to record:

1. Wages expense and withholdings (assume checks are written to the employees).
2. Employer tax liabilities.

Earnings = $4,500

FICA tax – OASDI on employees = 6.2%   *279 ee*

FICA tax – HI on employees = 1.45%   *65.25 ee*

FIT withheld from employees = $337.50 *ee*

FICA tax – OASDI on employers = 6.2%   *279 er*

FICA tax – HI on employers = 1.45%   *65.25 er*

FUTA tax = 0.8%   *36 er*

SUTA tax = 2.5%   *112.5 er*

2.6^2

2.1^{45}

Test 3

Congratulations! You have made it to the end of the book! Here is the final test. This is a cumulative test that will cover the entire accounting process that you have learned. Best wishes on your future endeavors. *ch. 9 - [posting?]*

Given the following information,

A. Create a general ledger for Mega Munch Corporation. *- chapter 9 (posting to a ledger) pg. 44-45*

B. Prepare journal entries for transactions and post them to the general ledger. *- ch. 7 (Journal entries + acc.) + ch. 6*

C. Prepare a bank reconciliation and any necessary journal entries, then post the journal entries to the general ledger. (Preparing cash receipts and cash disbursements journals may aid in this exercise, but is not required.) *? - ch. 14 Pg 82-83*

D. Prepare adjusting entries and post. *- chapter 11 (adjusting entries)*

E. Prepare a financial statement worksheet. *? Ch. 12 Pg. 69 + 70*

F. Prepare the 2004 financial statements: balance sheet, statement of retained earnings, multi-step income statement, and statement of cash flow. *Chapter 2 (balance sheet), ch. 3 (income state), ch. 4 (state. of retain earnings) ch. 5 (cash flow)*

G. Prepare closing entries and post. *Chapter 12 (closing entries)*
→ pg. 68 + 69
due nov 20th

B. use pg. 34 + 44
posting → pg. 45

Chapter 11 - is adjusting entries the same as adjusted trial balance? and what does P. mean by "post"?

Mega Munch Corporation
Chart of Accounts
(with balances as of 11/30/04)

Current Assets

		Debit	Credit
110	Cash	8,700	
111	Petty Cash	75	
112	Accounts Receivable	340	
113	Interest Receivable	0	
114	Inventory	600	
115	Purchase Discounts		20
116	Prepaid Advertising	400	
117	Marketable Equity Securities	3,000	
118	Allowance for Decline in Market Value		0
119	Bond Investment	5,000	

Property, Plant and Equipment

130	Delivery Van	10,000	
131	Accumulated Depreciation – Delivery Van		1,500

Current Liabilities

212	Accounts Payable		2,500
213	Advances from Customers		0
219	Salaries Payable		750
222	FICA Payable – OASDI		0
223	FICA Payable – HI		0
224	FIT Payable		0
225	FUTA Payable		0
226	SUTA Payable		0

Stockholders' Equity

310	Capital Stock, 1,000 shares issued		10,000
311	Retained Earnings		12,713
312	Dividends	0	

Income

410	Sales		42,000
411	Sales Returns & Allowances	120	
412	Sales Discounts	600	

Test 3

Jean Marinelli

Expenses

510	Cost of Goods Sold	20,000	
516	Advertising Expense	100	
517	Bank Fees	175	
518	Depreciation Expense	0	
519	Insurance Expense	300	
520	Miscellaneous Expense	110	
521	Office Supplies Expense	265	
522	Postage Expense	80	
523	Rent Expense	4,125	
524	Sales Salaries Expense	10,000	
525	Office Salaries Expense	4,000	
526	Payroll Tax Expense - Administrative	597	
527	Payroll Tax Expense - Sales	896	
530	Bad Debt Expense	0	

Other Revenues and Expenses

550	Cash Over and Short	0	
555	Interest Revenue		0
558	Unrealized Gain (Loss) on Securities		0

Transactions:

12-2	Paid $500 on account, check # 3240.
12-3	Purchased inventory on account – 20 units @ $20 each. A 3% discount is offered if paid within 10 days. Mega Munch uses the gross method of purchase discounts.
12-5	Bought office supplies for $50. Paid with check #3241.
12-6	Sold 4 units for $40 each on account. Mega Munch Corporation uses the LIFO method for inventory valuation. Terms are 2/10, net 30.
12-9	Received $220 on account.
12-11	Sold 6 units for $38 each in cash.
12-11	Paid for inventory purchased on 12-3, taking advantage of the discount, check #3242.
12-12	Received payment in full, less discount, from sale on 12-6.
12-14	Replenished petty cash fund, check #3243. There was $7.50 in the cash box and receipts as follows:

Office supplies $40.00
Postage   17.60
Misc. expenses   10.00

12-15	Sold 3 units on account for $40 each, terms: 2/10, net 30.
12-17	Customer returned 1 unit from sale on 12-6. Mega Munch is reimbursing the customer for the invoice amount less discount taken, check #3244.
12-18	Paid miscellaneous expenses of $125, check #3245.
12-18	Received $50 from a customer for a unit that must be special-ordered. The unit is expected to be received Jan. 3, 2005.
12-20	Paid salary (one sales employee), check #3246

Wages expense ($750 was recorded as payable on Nov. 30) $1,500
Withholdings:
FICA – OASDI $93.00
FICA – HI   2.18
FIT   100.00

12-20	Recorded employer taxes payable:

Matching FICA – OASDI & HI
FUTA – 0.8%
SUTA – 2.4%

12-21	It is determined that an amount due from customer of $120 is uncollectible. Mega Munch Corp. uses the direct write-off method.
12-23	Purchased 20 units of inventory on account for $19 each. Terms are 3/10, net 30.
12-26	Sold 3 units @$40 each for cash.
12-28	Bought office supplies for $35, check #3247.
12-29	Paid rent for month of $375, check #3248.
12-31	Paid payroll taxes and withholdings, check #3249.
12-31	Dividends of $600 were declared and paid. $120 to each shareholder with checks #3250, 3251, 32452, 3253, 3254.

bank statement

Community Bank
Statement of Account   Acct #0023001

Mega Munch Corporation   Statement Period:
4321 Main St.   From: Dec. 1, 2004
Somewhere, USA   Thru: Dec. 31, 2004

Beg. Balance	Total Withdrawals	Total Deposits	End. Balance
8959.50	2579.02	724.80	7105.28

Date	Withdrawals	Deposits	Transaction Description
12/09		220.00	Customer deposit
12/11		228.00	Customer deposit
12/12		156.80	Customer deposit
12/26		120.00	Customer deposit
12/31	20.00		Service charge

Detail of Checks Paid:

Check #	Date Paid	Amount	Check #	Date Paid	Amount
3238	12/01	135.00	3242	12/18	388.00
3239	12/06	74.50	3243	12/16	67.50
3240	12/10	500.00	3244	12/28	39.20
3241	12/11	50.00	*3246	12/24	1304.82

* Denotes check out of sequence.

Adjusting Entries:
1. 5% bonds were purchased on Sept. 1. Interest is paid Sept. 1 and March 1.
2. The value of the equity securities as of Dec. 31 is $2,900.
3. The delivery van was purchased in January of 2003 and has an expected life of 6 years with a salvage value of $1,000. Mega Munch Corporation uses straight-line depreciation and recognizes salvage value.
4. Magazine advertising was paid in advance for 1 year in October. The first of 4 issues came out in December.
5. Office employee wages earned in December, but not yet paid are $750.

Account balances as of January 1, 2004 (for preparation of cash flow statement). Note: the allowance for decline in market value is not taken into consideration for increases and decreases in asset values, since it is not necessarily a permanent increase or decrease in the value of the securities, as is depreciation to an asset such as delivery vans.

Current Assets		Debit	Credit
110	Cash	12,593	
111	Petty Cash	75	
112	Accounts Receivable	490	
113	Interest Receivable	0	
114	Inventory	1,500	
115	Purchase Discounts		0
116	Prepaid Advertising	300	
117	Marketable Equity Securities	3,000	
118	Allowance for Decline in Market Value		0
119	Bond Investment	0	

Property, Plant and Equipment

130	Delivery Van	10,000	
131	Accumulated Depreciation – Delivery Van		1,500

Current Liabilities

212	Accounts Payable		3,145
213	Advances from Customers		0
219	Salaries Payable		500
222	FICA Payable – OASDI		0
223	FICA Payable – HI		0
224	FIT Payable		0
225	FUTA Payable		0
226	SUTA Payable		0

Stockholders' Equity

310	Capital Stock, 1,000 shares issued		10,000
311	Retained Earnings		12,713
312	Dividends	0	

Resources

Following is a list of organizations and other information that will help get you started on the road to learning more about accounting.

Organizations

American Institute of Certified Public Accountants (AICPA) - www.aicpa.org

National Association of State Boards of Accountancy (NASBA) - www.nasba.org

Federal Accounting Standards Board (FASB) - www.fasb.org

State CPA societies each have their own websites. Do a search for your state and "CPA".

American Institute of Professional Bookkeepers (AIPB) - www.aipb.com

Publications

Accounting Today Magazine - www.electronicaccountant.com

www.businessweek.com

www.harvardbusinessonline.com

www.inc.com

www.wallstreetjournal.com

Other interesting sites

www.accountinginfo.com

www.bookkeeperlist.com

www.cpa2biz.com

www.cpaclass.com

www.cpemarket.com

Small Business Administation (SBA) - www.sba.gov

www.webcpa.com

Career search

www.monster.com

www.accounting.com

Search for your local newspaper online.

Keywords for online searches

Put two or more words together to look at different sites.

accountant

accounting

accounting software

bookkeeper

bookkeeping

cb - certified bookkeeper

cpa - certified public accountant

cma - certified management accountant

finance

Index

Thank you for purchasing this book!

We hope that you have enjoyed this book and that it has helped you in meeting your goals and that what you have learned will benefit you in your life pursuits.

Our complete line of books:

COMPLETE-A-SKETCH™ VOLUME 1 - ORTHOGAPHIC
COMPLETE-A-SKETCH™ VOLUME 2 - ISOMETRIC
COMPLETE-A-SKETCH™ VOLUME 3 - PERSPECTIVE
COMPLETE-A-SKETCH™ VISION - DEXTERITY - FOCUS™
PRACTICAL DRAFTING™
PRACTICAL GRAPHIC DESIGN™
PRACTICAL ACCOUNTING FUNDAMENTALS™

We are always working on new books, so please feel free to visit our website to see what new topics we may have added.

All the best,
Mel Peterman, Publisher
Insight Technical Education
www.insightteched.com
877.640.2256

1. a compound ~~journa~~ journal entry

2. a fiscal year

3. depreciation

4 adjusting entries

5. assets

6 D

7 H

8 A

9 B

10 ~~6~~ E

11 C

12 ~~D~~ F = G

13 I

14 H = F